Iowa's State Parks

Iowa's State Parks

Also
**Forests,
Recreation Areas,
and Preserves**

ROBERT CHARLES WOLF

 IOWA STATE UNIVERSITY PRESS / AMES

Robert Charles Wolf is a native Iowan and the author of *Fossils of Iowa* (Iowa State University Press, 1983).

Unless otherwise noted, photographs were taken expressly for this book by Kay Danielson.

First edition, 1991

Library of Congress Cataloging-in-Publication Data

Wolf, Robert Charles
    Iowa's state parks : also forests, recreation areas, and preserves / Robert Charles Wolf. — 1st ed.
        p. cm.
    Includes bibliographical references and index.
    ISBN 0-8138-1858-3 (cloth : alk. paper). — ISBN 0-8138-1857-5 (pbk. : alk. paper)
    1. Parks — Iowa — Guide-books. 2. Forest reserves — Iowa — Guide-books. 3. Recreation areas — Iowa — Guide-books. 4. Iowa — Description and travel — 1981 — Guide-books. I. Title.
F619.3.W65 1991
917.7704'33 — dc20   90–21361

Contents

Preface

AS I TRAVELED throughout Iowa gathering research for my earlier book, *Fossils of Iowa*, I frequently stopped at state parks along the way to break the monotony of driving. I soon became aware that Iowa has many beautiful parks where visitors can temporarily escape the problems of daily life. While there are numerous pamphlets available on individual parks and on the basic facts about the parks, and many parks have been the subjects of magazine or newspaper articles, some of this information is difficult to locate. Furthermore, there is no single source providing detailed information on all of the state parks. This book is intended to fill that need.

To assist readers of this book, each park description is split up into categories. A typical listing has the following categories:

LOCATION of the park with regard to roads and towns in the area

ADDRESS of the person or agency in charge of care for the park

TELEPHONE NUMBER of the ranger or agency

HISTORY in brief of the site before it became a park, how it became a park, and how it was developed

DESCRIPTION of the physical features of the park, including geology

FLORA AND FAUNA describing noteworthy plants and/or animals that can be seen there

ACTIVITIES offered in the park such as swimming, camping, hiking, fishing, etc.

ACKNOWLEDGMENT listing the person or persons who assisted in the research

FOR MORE INFORMATION directing readers to other publications concerning the park

The appendix section of the book also has sections on Iowa's geological and archaeological past.

Information for this book was compiled from newspapers; libraries; chambers of commerce; historical societies; the State Archives; publications of the Department of Natural Resources (formerly the Iowa Conservation Commission); the Geological Survey Bureau of the Department of Natural Resources (formerly the Iowa Geological Survey); county and regional historical books; *The Iowan; The Palimpsest; Annals of Iowa; Iowa Conservationist;* meeting minutes of the State Board of Conservations, the Iowa Fish and Game Commission, and the Iowa Conservation Commission; the *Proceedings of the Iowa Academy of Science;* unpublished works and reports; and other sources.

Many individuals assisted me in gathering information or have provided information. These include the staffs at the Fort Dodge Public Library and other libraries, wildlife management biologists, district foresters, area foresters, park rangers, county conservation officers and board directors; the staff at the Department of Natural Resources, the staff of the State Archives, and other individuals. Many of these people are individually acknowledged in the park descriptions.

Larry Wilson, Ross Harrison, Doyle Adams, and especially James Scheffler (all with the Department of Natural Resources) assisted me in my research. James Scheffler and others at the DNR reviewed the entire manuscript for clarity and accuracy, which I greatly appreciated. Rev. David Miller reviewed the chapter "Iowa's Archaeological Past," providing both support and criticism. Mr. Scheffler provided the photographs, and the DNR provided the park maps, for which I am grateful.

I wish to thank the staff at the Iowa State University Press for working with me on what turned out to be a five-year project.

Finally, I want to acknowledge the assistance of Milt Licht, who granted me access to a private collection of more than thirty years' worth of issues of the *Iowa Conservationist,* and of Mr. Licht's neighbor, Robert George, who towed my car out of the snow.

Introduction

IOWA'S STATE PARKS provides historical backgrounds and descriptions of the physical characteristics and facilities of Iowa's state-owned parks. This book focuses on the unique qualities of each park, features that the public can read about and experience.

- The reader will learn about Wilson Island Recreation Area, through which hundreds of thousands of geese migrate each autumn, and Lake Manawa State Park, which is one of Iowa's most popular parks with an attendance of a million visitors annually, nearly two million in 1984.
- In August 1804, the Lewis and Clark expedition camped on the bank of the Missouri River in an area that is today part of the Lewis and Clark State Park.
- Frank A. Gotch State Park was named in honor of the world heavyweight wrestling champion of the early 1900s. It was also the site of Fort Confederation, built by Frenchmen in the 1820s. Nothing remains of the fort today, however.
- Want to see a fire lookout tower? Visit Yellow River State Forest.
- Waubonsie State Park served as a hideout for Quantrill and his Confederate army during the Civil War. One of his members was Frank James, brother of Jesse.
- Maquoketa Caves State Park includes thirteen caves, one of which extends for more than 1,000 feet.
- Pillsbury Point State Park is where the Spirit Lake Massacre began. A total of forty settlers were killed in March 1857 by renegade Sioux Indians.
- In 1846 several hundred covered wagons made camp on the Mormon Trail at a site that today comprises Bobwhite State Park.
- Pikes Peak State Park was first visited by white men in June 1673 by the French explorers Marquette and Joliet.
- Pilot Knob State Park and Preserve contains Dead Man's Lake, where a small carnivorous plant lives, a relative of the Venus flytrap.

• At the butterfly garden at Bellevue State Park, visitors can view nearly thirty species of butterflies. The garden is capable of supporting sixty different species.

Actually, not all of the sites in this book are state parks. Some are state forests, others are state recreation areas, and still others are state preserves.

State parks offer a wide range of activities. Some offer no more than a picnic area where people can enjoy a leisurely few hours with nature. Other parks offer fishing, camping, picnicking, hiking, boating, winter activities, bridle trails, cabins and lodges for rental, concession stands, swimming, nature study, historical sites, scenic views, and more. Some of the state parks, such as Bigelow, Cold Springs, and Eagle Lake, are managed under long-term lease by county conservation boards. State parks are open every day of the year, weather permitting, from 4:00 A.M. until 10:30 P.M.

In addition to the parks, there are eight state-owned forests ranging in size from 33 acres to more than 9,000 acres. The larger forests offer many activities provided by state parks, and hunting is also permitted. The smaller forests have been left undeveloped and are primarily meant for research and preservation. The forests were set aside to ensure a continuous resource of timber and woodland habitat. They are open all year round. The forests include Backbone, Barkley, Gifford, Holst, Pilot Mound, Shimek, Stephens, Yellow River, and Loess Hills Pioneer State Forest in Monona and Harrison counties that is now in the acquisition stage.

Also included in this book are state-owned recreation areas. The largest recreation areas include Badger Creek, Brushy Creek, Mines of Spain, Pleasant Creek, Volga River, and Wilson Island. Recreation areas offer the public the widest range of outdoor activities possible (including hunting) without harming the natural setting. With the exception of Wilson Island, which is open from 4:00 A.M. until 10:30 P.M., these areas are open twenty-four hours a day all year. Brushy Creek, Mines of Spain, and Volga River are being developed. The DNR also manages a number of smaller recreation areas.

There are several state preserves in this book. These include Bixby State Park and Preserve, Brush Creek Canyon State Park and Preserve, Cayler Prairie, Fish Farm Mounds,

Fort Atkinson, Hayden Prairie, Kalsow Prairie, Pilot Knob State Park and Preserve, Sheeder Prairie, Turkey River Mounds, and Woodman Hollow.

There are more than sixty sites in the Iowa State Preserves System. Not all of the state preserves are state owned, however, and some have restricted access either because the owners requested so or because they have particularly sensitive habitats. The majority of the preserves are open to the public for activities that have the least effect on the habitat, such as nature study, hiking, and photography. Some of the preserves were set aside not for natural reasons but for their historical significance.

Because of the large number of sites already included, city, county, and federal lands were omitted from this book. In addition to the sites described in *Iowa's State Parks*, there are more than three hundred lesser known state-owned properties and more than three hundred county-owned parks. For information on these areas, readers can refer to the following publications of the Department of Natural Resources:

> *Preserving Iowa's Heritage, the Iowa State Preserves System*
> *Directory of State Preserves*
> *Iowa Public Hunting Areas*
> *County Conservation Area Directory*

This book is dedicated to my dad.

And to my writing friends,

whose encouragement made this book possible.

I hope that my encouragement will do the same for them.

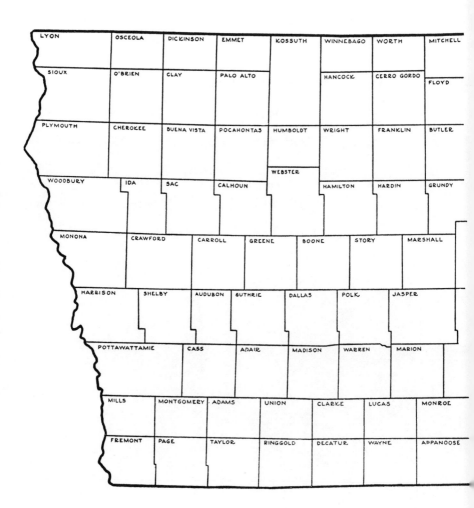

Iowa's State Parks

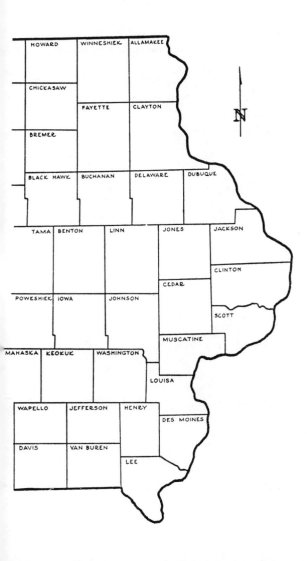

1 Northeast Iowa

(Opposite) *Julien Dubuque Monument seen from the mouth of Catfish Creek. Photograph by Dennis Magee. Used by permission.* (Above) *Scenic overlook of the city of Bellevue, the Mississippi River, and Lock and Dam 12 from Bellevue State Park.*

Potter's Mill, adjoining Bellevue State Park.

Rolling hills on the golf course at Wapsipinicon State Park.

Backbone State Park and Forest

LOCATION: 4 miles south of Strawberry Point on Highway 410 in Delaware County

ADDRESS: Dundee, Iowa 52038

TELEPHONE: (319) 924-2527

HISTORY: Backbone State Park was not always an area for recreation. Legends tell of Indian massacres and of criminals such as train robbers, cattle rustlers, horse thieves, and bank robbers hiding out here. However, as more and more settlers arrived in the area, the beauty of this place was revealed. Bobcats, timber wolves, and wild turkeys once thrived here.

Originally known as "Devil's Backbone" park, the growing popularity of the place prompted the state to purchase land totalling 1,200 acres from forty-four area citizens. Despite the reluctance of some landowners to sell, the land became Iowa's first state park. One of the landowners, Bert Bowers, sold an area known as Forestville, which included an old mill built by early settlers. The mill was destroyed by a flood only four years after the park was dedicated.

After two delays because of inclement weather, the park was formally dedicated on May 28, 1920, with five thousand people on hand. Its continuing popularity is apparent from the observation of the first caretaker, George Durham. He noted that over eight hundred people once visited the area in a single day.

Many of the park's facilities were built in the 1930s by the Civilian Conservation Corps.

DESCRIPTION: Today, Backbone State Park comprises 1,780 acres of hills and floodplains along the Maquoketa River. Bluffs of dolomitic limestone rise up to 100 feet above the river. They form a ridge nearly ¼ of a mile in length, which was originally called the "Devil's Backbone." The limestone was deposited during the Silurian Period, more than four hundred million years ago. Fossils can be seen in the rock, but collecting them is prohibited. The ridge is located in the central part of the park, with the Maquoketa River winding around both sides. There are exposures of this rock elsewhere in the park.

Within the park is one of Iowa's largest springs, Richmond Springs. With a temperature of 48°F, the spring flows at 2,300 gallons a minute and

Bluffs rising along the river at Wapsipinicon State Park.

7

fed the former fish hatchery in the northern part of the park. Visitors can also see a large boulder delicately balanced on a smaller rock, a handmade stone arch bridge, and a cave that extends for 300 feet. The cave, located in the northwestern part, narrows at first but then widens again.

The park is also the site of a 100-acre artificial lake formed by two dams on the river. The lake is about ¼ of a mile wide and 2½ miles long.

FLORA: In one area of the park is a hill where pine trees have been growing for at least two hundred years. Some of the trees have trunks over 3½ feet in diameter. These are among the oldest pines in the state. Also, to the south of the park is the Backbone State Forest, where more than fifteen varieties of trees grow.

In the spring, the park comes alive with more than a dozen species of wildflowers and ferns.

ACTIVITIES: Backbone State Park boasts five entrances; many miles of roads; 28 miles of trails; seven open shelters, each with a fireplace; a large lodge (with a two-hundred-seat auditorium) available for rental; eighteen cabins available for rental; and two campgrounds. One campground, located in the Forestville section of the park, was completed in 1968 and has 150 campsites. Thirty-two of the sites have electricity. The campground has modern restrooms, showers, and a playground. The other campground, located in the western part, has 64 nonmodern (no showers) campsites. A large playground was constructed in a popular picnic area in 1990.

Boating is permitted on the lake, but only electric motors are allowed. The lake, with a bathhouse, supervised beach, and concession stand, is located in the southeastern part of the park. The concession stand offers boat and boat motor rental, fishing gear, and other supplies. Also in the vicinity is a restaurant, the cabin area, a Boy Scout camp, and the Forestville campground.

In April 1990 the Iowa Civilian Conservation Corps Museum was opened, documenting the tremendous work of the CCC in the development of Iowa's state parks. It is located just within the park's west entrance.

Near the north entrance is the Backbone Country Club, featuring a nine-hole golf course open to the public, for which there is a charge. The state fish hatchery, on the park's north end, has a fish exhibit and a staff available to answer questions and provide information on fishing, particularly for trout.

Thousands of people visit Backbone State Park and Forest on a regular basis. Hiking is one of the most popular activities here, but bass and trout fishing are also popular. Snowmobiling is permitted on 18 miles of roads and trails, and on the lake when weather permits.

The forest covers 120 acres and offers squirrel and deer hunting.

- Trails blocked
  w/ trees - no bikes
- Campgrounds cleaned

- Trout fishing good

- Turkey river 25 min.
  219·245·1559 north
  good for canoe

- Trails blocked.
  w/ trees - no hikes
- Camp grounds closed

- Trout fishing good

- Turkey river 25 min.
  319 245-1564 north
  good for canoe

ACKNOWLEDGMENT: Craig Jackson, park ranger, Backbone State Park

FOR MORE INFORMATION:
Backbone State Park. Des Moines: Iowa Department of Natural Resources.
Tilden, F. The State Parks Their Meaning in American Life. New York: Alfred A. Knopf, 1962.

Beeds Lake State Park

LOCATION: 1 mile west of Hampton on Highway 3, then north 2 miles on a paved county road, in Franklin County

ADDRESS: Hampton, Iowa 50441

TELEPHONE: (515) 456-2047

HISTORY: In 1857 T. K. Hansberry built the first dike and gristmill here, forming the lake. The earthen dike across Spring Creek was more than 1,300 feet long and 10 feet high. The creek is fed by springs that flow year round. Before settlers arrived, this was a popular site among the Indians.

In 1864 William Beed purchased the property. He doubled the height of the dike and lengthened it to nearly 2,000 feet. He welcomed the public to use the lake and picnic areas free of charge. Beed died in 1903, and in 1904 the mill ceased to operate. In 1913 the dike was washed out.

Henry Pallus acquired the land on May 13, 1916. He had the old mill demolished in 1917 and drained the lake for pasture and farmland. Several Hampton residents, in an attempt to save the lake, tried to raise enough money to purchase the property. Not until 1933, when the Franklin County Izaak Walton League assisted in purchasing the land, did their efforts succeed. The land was donated to the state, and Beeds Lake State Park became a reality.

In the 1930s, the Civilian Conservation Corps did a great deal of work in the park. The main project was the construction of a dam from 1936–37. The dam has a spillway of 170 feet and natural rock walls 40 feet high of limestone of the Maynes Creek Formation, Mississippian Period. Water flowing over the dam is a beautiful sight. The park was officially opened to the public in 1938.

Over the years, the park grew in popularity. In 1964 a 100-foot-long

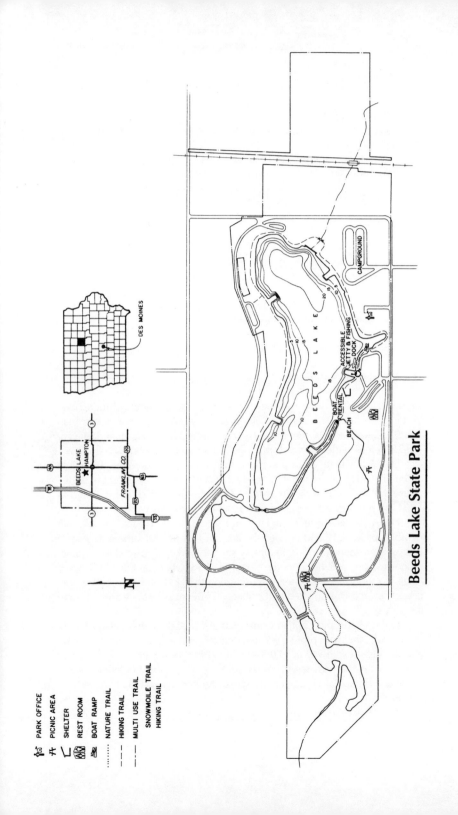

Beeds Lake State Park

Legend

- 🏠 PARK OFFICE
- ⚥ PICNIC AREA
- ⌐ SHELTER
- ⚥ REST ROOM
- 🚣 BOAT RAMP
- .... NATURE TRAIL
- — — HIKING TRAIL
- — · — MULTI USE TRAIL
- SNOWMOILE TRAIL
- HIKING TRAIL

BEEDS LAKE

ACCESSIBLE JETTY & FISHING DOCK

BOAT RENTAL

BEACH

CAMPGROUND

DES MOINES

BEEDS LAKE
HAMPTON
FRANKLIN CO

fishing dock was constructed, and in 1967 the old dike was improved. The new dike now serves as a walkway from the southeast to the northeast shores of the lake, with bridges on both ends to allow boat passage. The dike provides 650 yards of shore fishing.

However, during the late 1960s and early 1970s, the lake developed a silt buildup and an increase in the rough fish population. These caused a decline in fishing. To remedy the problem, the lake was drained, the rough fish were killed off with a chemical, and the lake bed was dredged to a depth of 23 feet. Restocking began in May 1972 with walleye, northern pike, largemouth bass, bluegill, and channel catfish.

DESCRIPTION: The dam is located on the west side of the lake. Foot trails ring the lake except for the western area. Snowmobile trails are located on the northwest and southwest sides of the lake. Picnic grounds, the campground, beach, boat ramp, and concession stand are all located on the lake's south side. There is a public access area on the northeast shore also. Visitors can walk completely around the lake.

ACTIVITIES: Today the 319-acre Beeds Lake State Park and the 100-acre lake offers 144 campsites (70 with electricity), modern restrooms and showers, picnicking, hiking, fishing, boating (10 HP limit on boat motors), snowmobiling, supervised swimming, and a playground. Boats and boat motors can be rented at the concession stand. The shore is tree-lined, and many species of waterfowl and shore birds can be seen.

The park also has a rustic shelter house that affords a scenic view of the lake. It is available to the public on a reservation basis. However, one of the most unusual features of this park is an airport located within walking distance, just south of the park entrance and across a country road.

ACKNOWLEDGMENT: John Ripperger, park ranger, Beeds Lake State Park

FOR MORE INFORMATION:
Beeds Lake State Park. Des Moines: Iowa Department of Natural Resources.

Bellevue State Park

LOCATION: 2½ miles south of Bellevue on Highway 52 in Jackson County

ADDRESS: R.R. 3, Box 184, Bellevue, Iowa 52031

TELEPHONE: (319) 872-3243, 872-4019

HISTORY: Marquette and Joliet passed through this area in June of 1673. One hundred sixty years later, in 1835, John D. Bell founded the town of Bellview here. Early documents show a variety of spellings. In March 1847, the council minutes changed from "Bellview" to "Bellevue." However, the precise origin of today's name and its spelling is unknown.

In the 1920s, the state acquired land that was known as South Bluff, and the park was officially opened to the public on August 24, 1928, with 4,500 people attending. Local citizens did considerable work to develop the park.

DESCRIPTION: The present-day Bellevue State Park comprises two units, the Nelson Unit and the Dyas Unit. The Nelson Unit marks the north end of the park and is situated among bluffs along the Mississippi River valley. One of these bluffs is 300 feet high and offers a spectacular view of the town of Bellevue. From other overlooks, visitors can view islands in the river, distant bluffs, wooded areas, and sand dunes along the river. The park's bluffs are comprised of shale of the Elgin Member of the Maquoketa Formation (Ordovician Period) and dolomitic limestones of the Silurian Period, Mosalem, Tete des Morts, and Blanding formations.

The Nelson Unit has 5 miles of numbered trails. The first trail leads to a scenic view of not only the town but Lock and Dam 12 and of an old mill known as Potter's Mill, built in 1843 on Mill Creek. The second trail provides access to three conical Indian burial mounds from the Woodland Culture (1000 B.C. to A.D. 1300). According to legend, one of the Indians buried here was a young squaw, Ma-ko-kee-ta, after whom the Maquoketa River was named. A third trail is recommended for joggers, cross-country skiers, and snowmobilers. It leads past food plots and areas planted to provide habitat for wildlife. The fourth trail provides access to an old limestone quarry that provided stone for the construction work in the park's early days. Most of the original buildings have been replaced. One of these is a lodge that is available to the public on a reservation basis.

The Dyas Unit is located 2 miles south of the Nelson Unit on Highway 52 and is also adjacent to the Mississippi River. It has 9 miles of trails, scenic views, an interpretive trail, and a stream where aquatic life can be viewed, including beavers at work. There is a fifty-two–site campground in this unit with modern restrooms and showers. Electricity is available at twenty-three of the sites.

FLORA AND FAUNA: A wide variety of wildlife is present, but the park is particularly popular among bird-watchers because of its many songbirds, including the pileated woodpecker, which can be seen in the timber along the river. This bird is nearly extinct in Iowa. Perhaps the best sight of all occurs in winter when bald eagles come to feed on dead or dying fish below Lock and Dam 12. As many as thirty of the birds can be seen at one time.

The park is home to several kinds of ferns, and an abundance of wildflowers can be found in the spring, especially hepatica and Jacob's ladder.

ACTIVITIES: Covering 547 acres, Bellevue State Park offers many picnic areas, five open shelters (which may be rented), a rental lodge, camping, scenic views, fishing, bird-watching, an interpretive trail, hiking, nature study, and a playground.

The Nelson Unit has a boat ramp near the south end that allows access to the Mississippi River. The backwater areas offer some of the best fishing in the state. Walleye fishing is especially good around April and May.

Snowmobilers can use all of the trails in the Dyas Unit as well as trails 3 and 4 in the Nelson Unit. The area is also open to cross-country skiing.

The South Bluff Nature Center is located in the Nelson Unit. The center is open afternoons on weekends and holidays and was originally a golf clubhouse. On display are artwork, Indian artifacts, paintings, minerals, and taxidermy work. The center also has a small library and offers programs for the family.

The park has a beautiful 1-acre butterfly garden, which is unique in Iowa and believed to be the largest of its kind in the Midwest. Within the first year of operation, the garden became home to twenty-eight species of butterflies. It is capable of supporting double that number.

ACKNOWLEDGMENT: Don Carrier, park ranger, Bellevue State Park

FOR MORE INFORMATION:
Bellevue State Park. Des Moines: Iowa Department of Natural Resources.

Jackson County's Scenic History Trail. Maquoketa: Jackson County Tourism Council.

Bixby State Park and Preserve

LOCATION: 2 miles north of Edgewood on a county road in Clayton County

ADDRESS: Backbone State Park, Dundee, Iowa 52038

TELEPHONE: (319) 924-2527 (Backbone State Park)

HISTORY: Bixby State Park and Preserve is a fragile area that has been studied by geologists and botanists for at least eighty years. The land was originally owned by W. J. Bixby of Edgewood. In October 1962, M. D. and Eva J. Flanders deeded 5 acres to the state. An additional 69 acres was purchased that same year by the state for eighteen hundred dollars. In 1978 an additional 115 acres on the west side of the preserve was acquired.

DESCRIPTION: The prominent feature in the 189-acre preserve is a dolomitic limestone cave from the Silurian Age among the wooded hills. The cave is one of only a very few in the Midwest in which the interior temperature remains around freezing. During the spring and summer, ice forms in the cave.

Also in the preserve are Bear Creek and several springs.

FLORA: Because of the cool temperature, the cave is home for a variety of unusual plants, including dwarf scouring rush, muskroot, ground pine, northern currant, and several rare lichens. Other areas of the preserve have a wide variety of wildflowers.

ACTIVITIES: The preserve offers hiking, picnicking, and nature study. No camping is allowed.

ACKNOWLEDGMENT: Anita J. Cox, librarian, Elkader Public Library

Brush Creek Canyon State Park and Preserve

LOCATION: 2 miles north of Arlington in Fayette County

ADDRESS: Volga River State Recreation Area, Fayette, Iowa 52142

TELEPHONE: (319) 425-4161 (Volga River State Recreation Area)

HISTORY: In the early 1930s, citizens of Arlington and nearby areas requested that the State Conservation Board consider some local land for the development of a state park. The land included Allen's Wildwood Springs, Pine Bluff, Brush Creek, and Moine Creek. Moine Creek gained popularity from gold that had been found there by pioneers. Brush Creek empties into the Volga River several miles to the north of the preserve. Both creeks converge in the area.

In 1934 four nearby communities (Arlington, Fayette, Oelwein, and West Union) raised funds to purchase the land and donate it to the state. The name of Brush Creek was selected because that was the original name for Arlington. The state park was rededicated as a state preserve in 1971.

DESCRIPTION: The preserve comprises 217 acres and includes bluffs of Silurian-Age dolomitic limestone up to 100 feet high. There is a steep valley with cedar trees along the top, which is located in the southwestern part. In the south central part is a rock chimney. The preserve's rough terrain contrasts with the gently rolling farmland to the south.

FLORA: The varying landscape is home to approximately 270 species of plants, including Canadian yew, shinleaf, bulbet fern, bladder fern, spikenard, and the only known occurrence of bearberry in the state.

ACTIVITIES: The preserve offers hiking trails, which are occasionally rugged, along Brush Creek in the central and southern parts of the preserve. Fishing is permitted in Brush Creek, which is a trout stream. The only roads are in the southern part, where the entrance is located. Also in this vicinity is a stone shelter that is open to the public on a first-come basis. Nearby are restrooms, a scenic bluff, and the picnic grounds. This is the only area of the preserve where picnicking is permitted. Brush Creek Canyon is also a popular area with bird-watchers.

ACKNOWLEDGMENT: Mona Ludwig, Fayette County Helpers Club and Historical Society, West Union

Cedar Rock

LOCATION: 3 miles northwest of Quasqueton off County Road W-35 in Buchanan County

TELEPHONE: (319) 934-3572

HISTORY: The site is a home designed for Lowell Walter and his family by Frank Lloyd Wright. Wright, a famous American architect, was born on June 8, 1867, and died on April 9, 1959. The home was built on a bluff of Devonian-Age Little Cedar and Coralville limestones overlooking the Wapsipinicon River. Wright began to design the home in 1945, and construction began in 1948. Two years later, the home was completed.

Lowell Walter died on August 1, 1981. The home was donated to the state in that year, and the estate provided $1.5 million for preservation and maintenance. The home has been extensively renovated and now appears as it was when the Walters lived there. Work is under way on a new visitor center.

DESCRIPTION: With more than 100,000 red bricks, walnut lumber, large picture windows, and at a cost of $100,000, the house sits on 11 acres of wooded land. The Garden Room has three glass walls that overlook the river and wooded valley. To provide outdoor lighting for guests, several miles of electrical wire were buried throughout the woods. Wright not only designed the residence but also its furnishings, down to the types of houseplants to be grown there. A visitor center was opened here in 1990.

ACTIVITIES: The house is open for tours to visitors from May through October, 11:00 A.M. to 5:00 P.M., Tuesday through Sunday.

ACKNOWLEDGMENTS: Dorothy Farber, librarian, Free Public Library, Independence
James Scheffler, Iowa Department of Natural Resources, Des Moines

FOR MORE INFORMATION:
Cedar Rock. Des Moines: Iowa Department of Natural Resources.

Clear Lake State Park

LOCATION: 2 miles south of Clear Lake on Highway 107 in Cerro Gordo County

ADDRESS: 2730 South Lakeview Drive, Clear Lake, Iowa 50428

TELEPHONE: (515) 357-4212

HISTORY: The town of Clear Lake was founded in 1871 by the merger of two nearby communities: Clear Lake City and Clear Lake Village. By the 1890s, amusement parks were located along the lakeshore. Before the settlers arrived, Indians fished and camped here.

Purchases of land at low cost from E. B. Stillman and beach property from C. F. Crane in 1924, along with additional beach purchases in 1925, formed Clear Lake State Park. Since then it has been necessary to increase the park's size to the present 102 acres to handle the increasing number of visitors. In 1938 the Works Progress Administration did work in the park, including the construction of a lodge near the beach that is still available to the public on a reservation basis.

DESCRIPTION: The state park is located on the southeast shore of Clear Lake. The spring-fed, 3,643-acre lake was formed by the retreating Des Moines Lobe of the Wisconsin Glacial Stage about fourteen thousand years ago.

Clear Lake State Park is one of the most heavily used parks in Iowa. An estimated thirty thousand campers come here yearly. This campground, combined with the nearby McIntosh Woods State Park campground, is one of the most popular state-owned camping areas in Iowa. Combined attendance of all visitors to these two parks is estimated at half a million people each year.

FLORA AND FAUNA: Because of the closeness to the Clear Lake–Mason City area, and because of the high number of visitors, wildlife has suffered somewhat in the park. Trees present include mature bur oak, ash, maple, and cottonwood. There are other areas around the lake that have more abundant wildlife.

ACTIVITIES: The park includes a 27-acre modern campground with 225 sites, 96 of which have electrical outlets. Modern restrooms and showers are provided. The park also has a 900-foot beach for swimming, a beautiful 25-acre picnic area, a rental lodge, a playground, and Woodford Island, a 2.9-acre forested island that rises up to 20 feet above the lake.

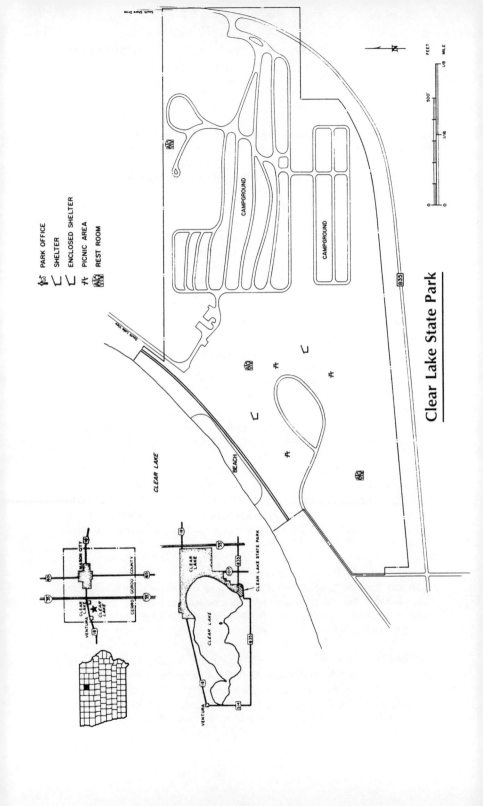

Clear Lake State Park

PARK OFFICE
SHELTER
ENCLOSED SHELTER
PICNIC AREA
REST ROOM

CAMPGROUND

CAMPGROUND

CLEAR LAKE

BEACH

South Shore Drive

South Lake Loop

FEET
MILE

Walleye, largemouth bass, smallmouth bass, crappie, northern pike, and bullhead are the common types of fish. The greatest concentration of yellow bass in the state occurs here, and there is also a good population of white bass. Although there is no boat ramp located inside the park, ramps are located elsewhere along the shore, and boat rental is available. There are no restrictions on horsepower for boat motors.

Snowmobiling is permitted in the area, and the lake and two nearby marshes are open to hunting.

Along the northeast shore is a DNR fisheries bureau facility owned and staffed by the state. There are many types of fish on display there.

ACKNOWLEDGMENTS: Jay Eason, Clear Lake State Park
Robert Schaut, park ranger, McIntosh Woods

FOR MORE INFORMATION:
Clear Lake. Clear Lake: Clear Lake Area Chamber of Commerce.
Clear Lake and McIntosh Woods State Parks. Des Moines: Iowa Department of Natural Resources.
Clear Lake State Park. Des Moines: Iowa Department of Natural Resources.

Echo Valley State Park

LOCATION: On east edge of West Union in Fayette County; bear east on paved County Road B-64 off of Highway 18, continue east for slightly more than a mile, then turn south and continue southward for slightly more than a mile.

ADDRESS: Fayette County Conservation Board, Fayette, Iowa 52142

TELEPHONE: (319) 425-3613 (Fayette County Conservation Board)

HISTORY: Around the turn of the century, the area became popular for picnicking and trout fishing. The park was dedicated in the early 1930s and was developed by the Civilian Conservation Corps and the Works Progress Administration between 1934 and 1936. A small artificial lake became popular with park users until the 1940s, when the lake developed an accumulation of silt and a structural flaw was discovered in the dam. Without the lake, the park's popularity quickly diminished. The buildings and picnic areas were swallowed up by the woods.

In 1984 the Iowa Conservation Commission turned over management of the park to the Fayette County Conservation Board. An ambitious restoration effort is under way at the park, and some of the structures that have been "discovered" are a flagstone walkway with a canopy of walnut trees, an unusual pyramid-shaped dam, limestone fireplaces in abandoned picnic areas, a limestone archway from the 1890s, and an old limestone kiln that provided building blocks used in the park's construction and in buildings in West Union. The park has a mysterious and ghostly atmosphere.

DESCRIPTION: Glover's Creek runs through the northern part of the park. Otter Creek meanders through the central and southern parts. In the eastern area of the park, the streams run along either side of a cherty dolomitic limestone bluff (Silurian Period, Hopkinton Formation). In some places, only 15 feet of rock separates the creeks. The two creeks converge immediately east of the park. Both are stocked with trout. There are trails throughout the southern half of the park. Picnic areas with shelters and restrooms can be found in the southwestern part. The entrance is located at the south end, and from there the road drops downhill. Fishing access is offered along Glover's Creek in the north and along Otter Creek in the south.

FLORA AND FAUNA: The park has an abundance of wildflowers, trees, shrubs, animals, and waterfowl.

ACTIVITIES: The 100-acre park offers picnicking, hiking, fishing, and primitive camping.

ACKNOWLEDGMENT: Laurie Engle, naturalist/ranger, Fayette County Conservation Board, Fayette

Fish Farm Mounds State Preserve

LOCATION: 4 miles south of New Albin on Highway 26 in Allamakee County

HISTORY: Around 250 B.C., the Hopewell Indian culture began to grow in what is now the Ohio area. They buried their dead in mounds overlooking rivers. Their villages spread westward as far as Kansas. Before their culture's decline around A.D. 400, they had left numerous mounds along the Mississippi River. The majority of the mounds were destroyed in the late 1800s by settlers who cleared the land for farming or collected artifacts.

The preserve was acquired by the state in 1920 from the Fish family.

DESCRIPTION: This 3-acre archaeological preserve has one of the few remaining Hopewell mound groups in the state. About thirty of the mounds are preserved on a ridge overlooking the Mississippi River. Bluffs of Jordan sandstone (Cambrian Period) can be seen near the tops of nearby hills. Older Cambrian deposits are also present.

ACTIVITIES: The preserve has trails for hiking and a parking area. Adjacent to the preserve is a wildlife area of 570 acres. Among the forested hills, deer, squirrel, grouse, turkey, and woodcock can be hunted.

Fort Atkinson State Preserve

LOCATION: Northern edge of Fort Atkinson off Highway 24 in Winneshiek County

ADDRESS: Volga River State Recreation Area, Fayette, Iowa 52142

TELEPHONE: (319) 425-4161 Volga River State Recreation Area

HISTORY: In the 1800s, the Winnebago Indians were ordered by the federal government to leave Wisconsin and settle in Iowa. This was necessary to open up that state for settlers. Once settled in Iowa, the peaceful Winnebagoes were frequently attacked by the more hostile Sioux and the Sac and Fox Indians.

In May 1840, under direction of Brigadier General Henry Atkinson, commander of the Jefferson Barracks at St. Louis, a unit was sent to the Turkey River area to establish a fort. It was believed that a fort would intimidate the warring Indians.

In 1842 the fort was opened on a bluff overlooking the Turkey River and was named in honor of General Atkinson. A 12-foot-high stockade was erected, and several buildings were built from limestone in the area. This limestone is now known as the Fort Atkinson Member of the Maquoketa Formation, Ordovician Period.

Construction inside the fort continued until 1845. The buildings included four barracks, two of wood and two of stone. One of the stone barracks contained the hospital, chapel, and school. The other stone barrack housed the officers and their families. The soldiers lived in the two wooden barracks. Stone cannon houses were built on the northeast and southeast corners of the fort. Each housed two cannon. By the time the fort was completed, the cost was thirty-eight thousand dollars, which was fifteen thousand dollars higher than anticipated.

In 1846 the federal troops were called away from the fort to fight in the Mexican War. Notable people who served at, or were involved with, the fort included Schuyler Hamilton (Alexander Hamilton's grandson), Alexander McGregor (founder of the town of McGregor), and Jefferson Davis. When the federal troops left, the fort was manned by Iowa's first volunteer state soldiers. In 1848 the Winnebago Indians were again uprooted by the federal government and moved to Fort Snelling in Minnesota. In 1849 Fort Atkinson was abandoned.

In the 1930s, the state acquired the fort. The only remaining structures were the two stone cannon houses, part of the north stone barrack, the powder magazine, and a blockhouse. Work in the fort grounds from 1939 to 1941 revealed the location of the stockade and the foundations of some of the old buildings.

In 1958 reconstruction work began in the fort at a cost of forty-eight thousand dollars. On May 20, 1962, Fort Atkinson was officially dedicated as a state preserve.

DESCRIPTION: Today the 5-acre historical, geological, and archaeological preserve has a museum, which is located in the north barrack. On display are artifacts, maps, sketches, weapons, tools, and personal effects of the soldiers. The museum is open in the summer and early autumn.

ACTIVITIES: In addition to the museum, which is open seasonally, interpretive signs are located around the fort.

Each autumn, since 1973, the Fort Atkinson Rendezvous has been held. The rendezvous is reminiscent of the original rendezvous, which gave early trappers and settlers the opportunity to mingle and trade. The community, the Department of Natural Resources, and the Iowa State Preserves Advisory Board all sponsor the event. Dress, life-styles, sports activities, meals, and other aspects of the 1840s are recreated.

George Wyth Memorial State Park

LOCATION: In Cedar Falls on Highway 218, immediately south of the Cedar River, turn east on 1st Street (also known as Broadway), continue east for about 1 mile to the park. The park is in both Cedar Falls and Waterloo, in Black Hawk County.

ADDRESS: R.R. 2, Waterloo, Iowa 50701

TELEPHONE: (319) 232-5505

HISTORY: The first settlers here were William and Nancy Fisher in 1853. They raised five daughters and four sons in a log cabin near a lake that was later named in their honor. In 1875 they purchased 45 acres in this area from the state.

The park was dedicated in 1940 as the Josh Higgins Parkway but was renamed George Wyth Memorial in 1956, after a prominent businessman and conservation supporter from Cedar Falls.

DESCRIPTION: The developed sections of the 494-acre park are located to the south of the road. North of the road is a wildlife refuge.

The 51-acre George Wyth Lake was constructed in the early 1970s (enlarged to 90 acres in 1988) and is located in the eastern part of the park. The 38-acre natural Fisher Lake is a narrow body that meanders through the central and western areas of the park. The Cedar River flows along the southern part of the park. The Sac and Fox Indians called the river "Mosk-Wah" or, roughly, "Red Cedar River."

George Wyth Memorial State Park was renovated in 1980 and 1981. The development of new highways nearby also resulted in major changes to the park, including new land and water areas.

FLORA AND FAUNA: The park is part of a floodplain forest. Red cedar trees line the riverbanks. Wildlife is abundant, including a large deer population. Some rare plants and animals can be found here. The area has become popular with bird-watchers since more than 180 species of birds have been recorded here, including the pileated woodpecker, wood duck, and red-tailed hawk. Wildflowers are common in the spring, including the woodland phlox.

The George Wyth Nature Trail shows visitors many of the trees and shrubs present in the park.

ACTIVITIES: Largemouth bass can be caught in George Wyth Lake, but only electrical trolling motors are permitted. Sailboating on the lake has become popular, and there is a boat ramp.

23

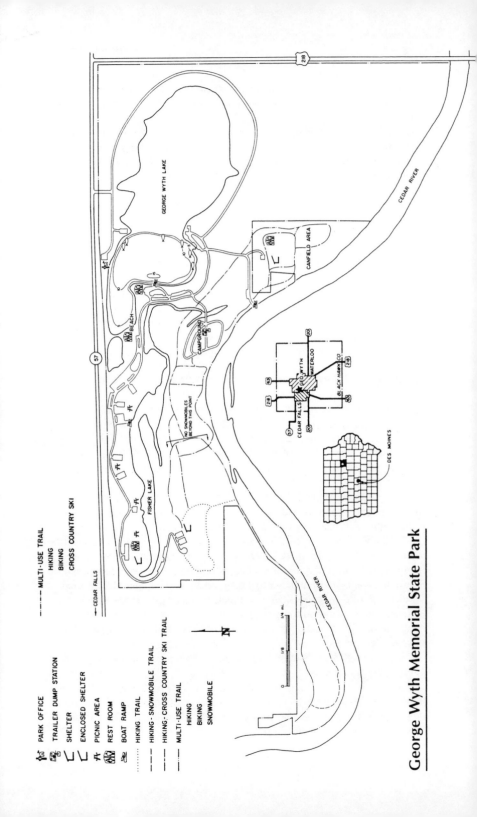

George Wyth Memorial State Park

Catfish and bullheads can be caught on Fisher Lake, and a boat ramp is available. Catfish, walleye, northern pike, and carp can be caught in the river; boat ramps provide access.

There is a 64-unit campground (43 have electricity) with modern restrooms and showers. Picnicking, bird-watching, hiking, a large playground, supervised swimming, a nature trail, a rental shelter, snowmobiling, and boat rental are also offered.

There is an excellent multipurpose trail linked to nearby Cedar Falls that is especially popular for bicycling. The park also offers some of the best cross-country skiing in northeastern Iowa.

ACKNOWLEDGMENT: Staff at George Wyth Memorial State Park

FOR MORE INFORMATION:
George Wyth Memorial State Park. Des Moines: Iowa Department of Natural Resources.
George Wyth Nature Trail. Des Moines: Iowa Department of Natural Resources.

Hayden Prairie State Preserve

LOCATION: 3½ miles south of Chester on County Road V-26 in Howard County

HISTORY: This prairie was owned by the same family for seventy-eight years. When the state purchased it in 1945 at a cost of $10,001, it became Iowa's first prairie preserve. The preserve was named to honor Dr. Ada Hayden, who was a professor of botany at Iowa State University. An estimated 30 million acres of prairie covered the state when the first settlers arrived. Today there are only about 1,000 acres of virgin prairie left in Iowa. This prairie was designated a national natural landmark in 1966 and was dedicated as a state preserve in 1968.

DESCRIPTION: This is the largest native prairie remaining in Iowa. One hundred forty acres are upland prairie, and 100 acres are intermediate and lowland prairie.

The prairie is separated into nine sections by paths that are mowed periodically. These paths serve as hiking trails and as fire lines. Small sections are burned on a rotating basis in the early spring. It has been demonstrated that controlled fires are beneficial to prairies. Burning removes debris, productivity is increased, and the plants are generally more vigorous. Only small areas are burned at a time to enable wildlife to escape to other areas of the prairie.

FLORA: Hayden Prairie is home to 150 plant species. Some of the prairie grasses reach heights of 8 feet. Wildflowers are abundant, including pasqueflower, shooting star, white prairie clover, purple prairie clover, meadow rue, leadplant, wild strawberry, oxeye, loosestrife, wild indigo, and prairie rose.

ACTIVITIES: The prairie offers nature study and pheasant, deer, rabbit, and woodcock hunting.

ACKNOWLEDGMENT: Jim Ripple, wildlife management biologist, Decorah

Julien Dubuque Monument

LOCATION: In the southeastern part of Dubuque (Dubuque County). From the intersection of Highways 61 and 52, go south on 52 for 2 miles to Old Massey Road. Then turn left to the entrance of the Mines of Spain State Recreation Area. The monument is located in the northeastern part of the recreation area.

HISTORY: The first white man in the area is believed to have been Nicholas Perrot, a Frenchman. In the 1690s, he discovered lead deposits here and operated the first lead mines, teaching the technique of lead mining to local Indians.

In the 1750s, Jean Marie Cardinal, another Frenchman, settled here, near the mouth of the Wisconsin River. The hunter and trapper, originally from Canada, visited the lead mines frequently in the 1760s and 1770s. He also made several trips to St. Louis to sell furs. His wife, Carechi-Coranche (Mary Ann), was a Pawnee Indian. Cardinal, supposedly, is the only Iowan to die in the Revolutionary War. According to legend, in 1780 he arrived in St. Louis with news of a pending British attack. The village was able to mount a successful defense, but one of the casualties was Cardinal.

In that same decade, another Frenchman from Canada settled on the Iowa side of the river. He was Julien DuBuque. He is the first known permanent settler in Iowa. With the permission of the Spanish who claimed the land, and under an agreement with the Fox Indians, DuBuque began to mine lead in 1788. The mines would later be called the Mines of Spain, and the community that was founded here was called Dubuque.

DuBuque married Petosa, daughter of Chief Peosta of the Fox Indians. Before he died in 1810, his mines were producing 400,000 pounds of lead annually. He was buried by the Indians. Chief Peosta died in 1814 and was buried next to DuBuque. In the 1850s, lead production declined drastically in the mines.

In 1897 a 28-foot-high stone monument was erected in memory of DuBuque. His body was reburied under the monument, which is located at the mouth of Catfish Creek on the Mississippi River. However, it was not until 1973 that the remains of his wife, Petosa, and his father-in-law, Chief Peosta, were given proper burials alongside DuBuque.

The land was acquired by the state in the 1930s at the request of the American Legion.

ACTIVITIES: The 12-acre area has facilities for picnicking and offers a scenic view of the Mississippi River and of the Mines of Spain. For more information, refer to the Mines of Spain State Recreation Area.

ACKNOWLEDGMENTS: Mike Abel, park ranger, MInes of Spain State Recreation Area
Staff at the Iowa Department of Natural Resources

Maquoketa Caves State Park

LOCATION: 6 miles northwest of Maquoketa on Highway 428 in Jackson County

ADDRESS: R.R. 2, Maquoketa, Iowa 52060

TELEPHONE: (319) 652-5833

HISTORY: The first white men known to have seen the caves were Joshua Bear and David Scott, around 1834. They were hunting deer in the area and had trapped some of the animals in a canyon. Somehow, in a snowstorm, the deer escaped. While the hunters searched for the escape route, they discovered the lower entrance to a large cave now known as Dance Hall Cave.

Indians knew of the caves and inhabited them as early as ten thousand years ago. The Woodland Indians used the caves during winter around two

Maquoketa Caves State Park

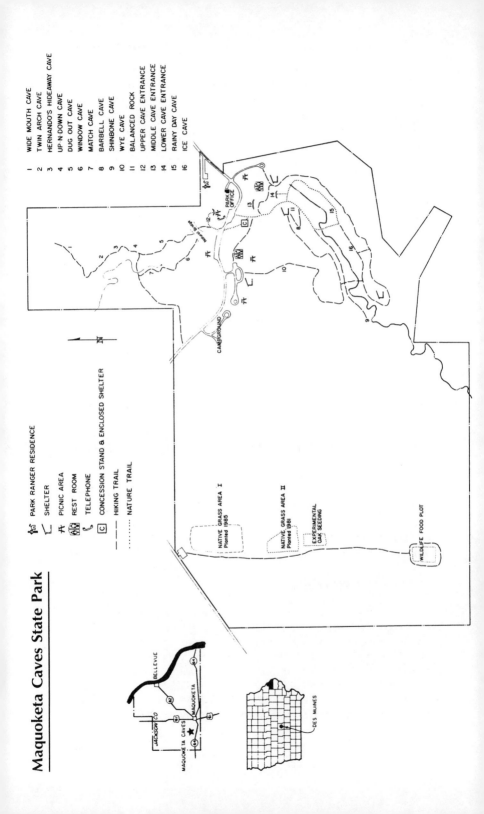

1 WIDE MOUTH CAVE
2 TWIN ARCH CAVE
3 HERNANDO'S HIDEAWAY CAVE
4 UP-N-DOWN CAVE
5 DUG OUT CAVE
6 WINDOW CAVE
7 MATCH CAVE
8 BARBELL CAVE
9 SHINBONE CAVE
10 WYE CAVE
11 BALANCED ROCK
12 UPPER CAVE ENTRANCE
13 MIDDLE CAVE ENTRANCE
14 LOWER CAVE ENTRANCE
15 RAINY DAY CAVE
16 ICE CAVE

PARK RANGER RESIDENCE
SHELTER
PICNIC AREA
REST ROOM
TELEPHONE
CONCESSION STAND & ENCLOSED SHELTER
HIKING TRAIL
NATURE TRAIL

NATIVE GRASS AREA I
Planted 1985

NATIVE GRASS AREA II
Planted 1981

EXPERIMENTAL
OAK SEEDING

WILDLIFE FOOD PLOT

PARK OFFICE

CAMPGROUND

JACKSON CO.
BELLEVUE
MAQUOKETA
MAQUOKETA CAVES

DES MOINES

thousand years ago. Later, the Sac and Fox Indians held council meetings here. Indian pottery, arrowheads, and spears have been discovered.

In the early 1930s, the Federated Women's Club and other citizens in Maquoketa urged the state to develop a state park here. They suggested the name of Morehead Caves State Park. The park was dedicated on October 13, 1933. Development in the park was carried out by the Civilian Conservation Corps from 1933 to 1936 and by the Works Progress Administration from 1938 to 1941.

DESCRIPTION: With at least thirteen caves, Maquoketa Caves State Park (266 acres) has more caves than any other state park in Iowa. Several of the caves are more than 30 feet long, with the longest being more than 1,000 feet.

The park has less than ½ mile of paved road but more than 6 miles of hiking trails. The trails provide access to many geological features. Some of the trails are rugged. In addition to the caves and sinkholes, a huge natural bridge, balanced rocks, and high bluffs can be seen. In the center of the park are bluffs up to 75 feet high offering scenic views. The natural bridge was at one time a cave entrance. Today it stands nearly 50 feet above Raccoon Creek. The creek meanders through the major caves. Near the lower entrance of Dance Hall Cave is a 17-ton boulder balanced on a 1-foot-wide rock base.

The caves, most of the hiking trails, and an interpretive trail can be found in the eastern part of the park. The major caves are lighted, but the smaller caves require flashlights. Visitors are urged to stay on the trails and not explore for possibly undiscovered caves. All of the caves are marked. These include:

Dance Hall Cave: the largest of the caves, it was used many years ago for square dances. At one time, the cave probably extended for more than 5,000 feet to the Maquoketa River. Erosion has caused cave-ins, and today the cave is about 1,100 feet in length. A flood destroyed the cave's original walkways, but prisoners from the Men's Reformatory in Anamosa renovated the cave in 1982–1983. A concrete walkway and lighting enhance the experience of cave exploring.

Bats Passage: so named because the cave's ceiling is a popular hibernation site for bats during the winter. The interior temperature remains around 50°F year round.

Devil's Cavern: a sinkhole leading to a cave. Another sinkhole is located below Fat Man's Misery and provides visitors with a cross-sectional view of the natural depression.

Ice Cave: cooler than the other caves. Geologists believe that ice is present somewhere in the cave, which cools the air.

Rainy Day Cave: 130 feet long with a constant temperature of 55°F.

29

Other caves are Fat Man's Misery, Wide Mouth Cave, Twin Arch Cave, Up-N-Down Cave, Dug Out Cave, Match Cave, Tourist Delight, Barbell Cave, Wye Cave, Hernando's Hideaway, Window Cave, Shinbone Cave, and Steel Gate Passage, in which to enter visitors must crawl for 800 feet.

The majority of the caves and sinkholes were formed by running water. A few of the caves, such as Fat Man's Misery, were formed by shifting rocks and are known as mechanical caves. The caves have been opened up in dolomitic limestone of the Silurian period, Hopkinton formation. Stalactites and stalagmites were present in the larger caves but were removed years ago by visitors. Stalactites are forming again in Devil's Cavern at a rate of an inch per century. Visitors are asked not to touch the stalactites because their formation will be halted. During the winter, large icicles form on the ceiling and floor and mimic stalactites and stalagmites.

FLORA AND FAUNA: The park is home to more than 350 species of plants, including some rare or endangered species. The varieties of flora and fauna found here are not surpassed by any other state park. Uncommon trees found in the heavily wooded park include chinquapin oak and largetooth aspen. Some of the wildlife found here include coyote, red and gray fox, and white-tailed deer. Bobcats have been observed in the park but are very rarely seen by the public.

ACTIVITIES: At present, the park has a 29-site nonmodern campground. It is located in the north central area. (A modern campground with electricity and showers is planned for 1991–92.) Also present is a concession stand and picnic area. In addition to hiking and scenic views, spelunkers frequently come to explore the caves, and mountain climbers use the park for practice.

A trail in the western area of the park takes hikers past a native prairie, an experimental oak nursery, and a wildlife food plot.

Near the park is the Sagers Museum. Inside the stone building are displayed many Indian artifacts, as well as a variety of pioneer items. The museum is managed by the DNR and is open on a seasonal basis.

ACKNOWLEDGMENT: Larry Zirkelbach, park ranger

FOR MORE INFORMATION:
The Caves Trail. Des Moines: Iowa Department of Natural Resources.

Jackson County's Scenic Historic Trail. Maquoketa: Jackson County Tourism Council.

Maquoketa Caves State Park. Des Moines: Iowa Department of Natural Resources.

McIntosh Woods State Park

LOCATION: ¾ of a mile east of Ventura on Highway 18 in Cerro Gordo County

ADDRESS: Ventura, Iowa 50482

TELEPHONE: (515) 829-3847

HISTORY: In 1934 the first 60 acres of the McIntosh Woods State Park was purchased. Today the park and adjacent McIntosh Wildlife Management Area cover 278 acres along the northwest shore of Clear Lake.

DESCRIPTION: The park has gently sloping woods and meadows. It is one of the few areas along the lakeshore that has not been privately developed. McIntosh Woods State Park and the nearby Clear Lake State Park attract half a million visitors annually.

Clear Lake is a glacial lake. Glacial till of the Nebraskan, Kansan, and Wisconsin glacial stages are present.

FLORA AND FAUNA: The park has a wide variety of trees, shrubs, and wildflowers, some of which are rare. Notable wildflowers include wild spikenard, jewelweed, and several species of asters.

Many species of mammals can be found here. The area is also rich in gulls, shore birds, and many kinds of frogs.

ACTIVITIES: There is a 45-site campground with modern restrooms, showers, and electricity. Also offered are boating and fishing in the 3,684-acre Clear Lake, hiking, a nature trail, and picnicking. A boat ramp with extensive parking areas provides good lake access. An unsupervised swimming area is located on the west side of a peninsula on the lake. Boat rental is available nearby. There is no size restriction on boat motors. For more information, see Clear Lake State Park.

The McIntosh Wildlife Management Area offers waterfowl, pheasant, and deer hunting. It is composed mainly of upland habitat with some marsh areas. Waterfowl hunting is also permitted on the lake and in a few other areas along the lakeshore.

ACKNOWLEDGMENT: Robert Schaut, park ranger, McIntosh Woods State Park

FOR MORE INFORMATION:
Interpretive Trail Guide: McIntosh Woods State Park. Des Moines: Iowa Department of Natural Resources.

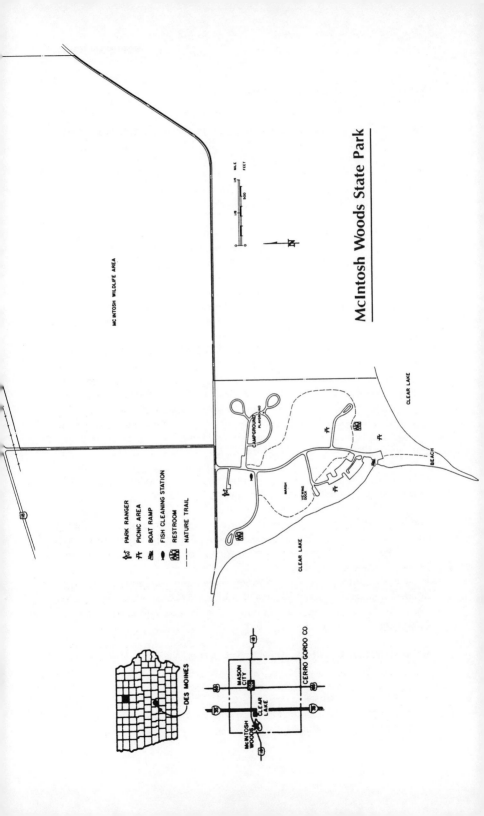

McIntosh Woods State Park

MC INTOSH WILDLIFE AREA

PARK RANGER
PICNIC AREA
BOAT RAMP
FISH CLEANING STATION
RESTROOM
NATURE TRAIL

CAMPGROUND
PLAYGROUND

MARSH

VIEWING DECK

CLEAR LAKE

CLEAR LAKE

BEACH

MILE
FEET

DES MOINES

MASON CITY

CLEAR LAKE

McINTOSH WOODS

CERRO GORDO CO

Mines of Spain State Recreation Area

LOCATION: In the southeastern part of Dubuque (Dubuque County). From the intersection of Highways 61 and 52, go south on 52 for 2 miles to Old Massey Road. Then turn left to the entrance.

ADDRESS: R.R. 2, Old Bellevue Road, Dubuque, Iowa 52001

TELEPHONE: (319) 556-0620

HISTORY: Evidence of Indian habitation at least five thousand years ago has been found in this area. This represents either the Archaic or early Woodland cultures. Burial mounds of this age are present. Later a Fox (Mesquakie) Indian village existed here, the second largest known Fox village. In the 1600s, French trappers discovered lead here and showed the Indians how to mine it.

In the late 1700s, Julien DuBuque became the first permanent white settler in Iowa. He became friendly with the Indians and was allowed to mine the lead, which he shipped to St. Louis on the Mississippi River (see Julien Dubuque Monument). Some of the lead was said to have been used by George Washington's army during the Revolutionary War. DuBuque died in 1810, but the Indians kept the mines operating until 1832 when the Black Hawk treaty opened up the land to settlers. At one time, 10 percent of the world's lead came from the mines, but production declined in the late 1800s and the mines were finally closed in 1936. Remnants of the once flourishing mining activity may still be seen in the area.

Another noted settler was Otto Junkermann, a German, who arrived in Dubuque shortly after the Black Hawk treaty and became a prominent druggist.

The land has changed hands several times during its history—first France owned it, then Spain, England, and France again when it was sold to the United States as part of the Louisiana Purchase in 1803.

DESCRIPTION: Acquired by the state in 1980, the Mines of Spain is considered to be one of the most unique properties in the state park system. The acquisition of the 1,300 acres of forest involved the U.S. Department of the Interior, the Iowa Natural Heritage Foundation (a private organization), and the Iowa Conservation Commission (now the Department of Natural Resources). A substantial donation was made by landowners Herman and Marcella Lott. Portions of the area are included in, or border on, part of the Upper Mississippi River National Wildlife Refuge.

The nineteenth-century Junkermann farm has been partially restored and is located in the northeastern area of the Mines of Spain, near the E. B. Lyons Nature Center. Present on the old farmstead is a private chapel built

33

from pinewood by Junkermann in 1861. It is considered to be one of his best projects and is a popular attraction.

Also present in the area are thickly wooded valleys, numerous caves believed to be millions of years old, and exposures of shale, limestone, and dolomitic limestone. The Ordovician-Period Dunleith, Wise Lake, Dubuque, and Maquoketa formations are represented. An old limestone quarry is also present, but visitors should beware of falling rock.

Located along the Mississippi River and along Catfish Creek, the area also includes the Julien Dubuque Monument in the northeastern part and the E. B. Lyons Nature Center in the northwestern part. The nature center was built by the city of Dubuque with funds donated by Mr. E. B. Lyons. The state acquired the center by long-term lease in 1983 and uses it as a conservation education center to inform the public of the significant natural, historic, and archaeological features of the Mines of Spain State Recreation Area. Large picture windows overlook the forest, and there are hiking trails in the area. Other parts of the Mines of Spain include Cattisse Hollow Access in the southern part and the Catfish Creek Access in the northern part.

FLORA AND FAUNA: The area includes one of the best examples of an oak-hickory forest in the state. At least 480 species of plants have been identified, including trees, shrubs, wildflowers, prairie grasses, mosses, and liverworts.

The Mines of Spain State Recreation Area also has a wide variety of animal life: amphibians; reptiles; at least forty-three species of mammals, including bobcats and otters; and numerous birds, including bald eagles in the winter. The area also provides one of the very few nesting places in the state for the red-shouldered hawk.

ACTIVITIES: At present, the MInes of Spain offers a variety of displays and programs at the E. B. Lyons Nature Center, nature study, scenic views, photography, hiking, bow hunting, and trapping.

ACKNOWLEDGMENT: Mike Abel, park ranger, Mines of Spain State Recreation Area

FOR MORE INFORMATION:
Mines of Spain. Des Moines: Iowa Department of Natural Resources.
Trail Stops to Listen and Look By: A Nature Center Brochure. Des Moines: Iowa Department of Natural Resources.

Palisades-Kepler State Park

LOCATION: 3½ miles west of Mount Vernon off Highway 30 in Linn County

ADDRESS: R.R. 2, Mount Vernon, Iowa 52314

TELEPHONE: (319) 895-6039

HISTORY: For the famed poet Carl Sandburg, the "Palisades" was a favorite recreational area in the 1920s and 1930s. The vacation area was first developed around the turn of the century by James Minott. Covering 160 acres, the resort included a hotel, restaurant, general store, boathouse, and private lots for cabins. A few hundred people lived here.

In 1922 the state acquired 140 acres of floodplain, upland forest, and bluffs (palisades). In 1926 the Louis Kepler Memorial Area was added to the park. Development in the park was done between 1934 and 1937 by the Civilian Conservation Corps. The CCC was a program intended to provide Americans with jobs during the Depression.

DESCRIPTION: Today Palisades-Kepler State Park covers 840 acres along both sides of the Cedar River, but only the east side has been developed for the public.

The palisades are dolomitic limestone bluffs rich in fossils that tower up to 75 feet above the river. The bluffs represent Silurian-Period Scotch Grove and Gower formations.

Indian burial mounds can be found in the north central area of the park. The south central part has a nature study area. In the west central part is a nature trail to the west of the campground and pleasant scenic views of the river and surrounding land.

FLORA: A wide variety of wildflowers grow in the park, and the area is thickly forested.

ACTIVITIES: The Cedar River offers many kinds of fish, with channel catfish and flathead catfish, some of which are quite large, being the most popular. The park offers picnicking, snowmobiling, unsupervised swimming, cross-country skiing, and a 76-site campground. The campground has modern restrooms, showers, and 45 electrical hookups. A rustic lodge and four cabins are available to the public on a rental basis.

ACKNOWLEDGMENT: Park ranger, Palisades-Kepler State Park

FOR MORE INFORMATION:
 Palisades-Kepler State Park. Des Moines: Iowa Department of Natural Resources.

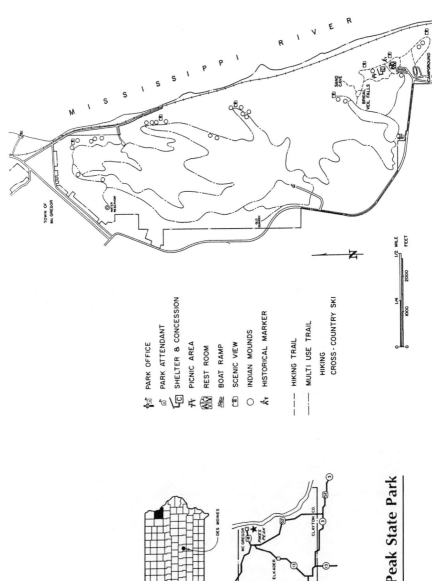

MISSISSIPPI RIVER

TOWN OF McGREGOR

PARK OFFICE
PARK ATTENDANT
SHELTER & CONCESSION
PICNIC AREA
REST ROOM
BOAT RAMP
SCENIC VIEW
INDIAN MOUNDS
HISTORICAL MARKER

HIKING TRAIL
MULTI USE TRAIL
HIKING
CROSS - COUNTRY SKI

DES MOINES

McGREGOR
PIKES PEAK
ELKADER
CLAYTON CO.

Pikes Peak State Park

Pikes Peak State Park

LOCATION: 3 miles south of McGregor on Highway 340 in Clayton County

ADDRESS: McGregor, Iowa 52157

TELEPHONE: (319) 873-2341

HISTORY: With the highest cliff on the Mississippi River, Pikes Peak State Park was named after Zebulon Pike, who explored the upper Mississippi River in 1805 for the U.S. Government.

The first white men known to have seen Pikes Peak were Louis Joliet and Father Jacques Marquette. On June 17, 1673, they sailed out of the Wisconsin River to begin their exploration of the Mississippi River.

Originally known as the "Munn Site," the land was acquired by the state from the federal government.

DESCRIPTION: Covering 970 acres, the park is part of the Upper Mississippi River National Wildlife Refuge. Along the river are bluffs up to 500 feet high exposing sandstone, limestone, shale, and dolomitic limestone of the Ordovician Period. Formations represented include the Oneota, Shakopee, Saint Peter, Platteville, Decorah, and Dunleith. The bluffs offer scenic views of the Mississippi and Wisconsin rivers and the towns of Marquette, McGregor, and Prairie du Chien. Point Ann in the northern part of the park offers an excellent view of McGregor.

The park has Indian effigy mounds in the central and southern areas. Also in the southern area is a campground with electricity and modern facilities, picnic areas, a scenic stone shelter and concession stand, Bridal Veil Falls, the Pikes Peak overlook area, and Sand Cave, which displays colorful sandstone. Near the picnic area, two overlook structures provide breathtaking views of the river valley.

There are 7 miles of hiking trails in the park, including a series of steps, walkways, and viewing platforms. One trail leads from Pikes Peak to Bridal Veil Falls, a drop of 500 feet. There are no roads through the park, but roads do provide access to the ranger's residence in the western part, Point Ann in the northern part, and the campground and Pikes Peak overlook area in the southern part. There are parking areas at these three locations.

FLORA AND FAUNA: Oak and maple trees are common in the park, and in the spring, the park's many wildflowers are in full bloom. The park also has a wide variety of birds. Pikes Peak is especially beautiful during the fall leaf-color season.

ACTIVITIES: The campground has 75 sites with modern restrooms, showers, and electricity. Also offered are hiking, picnicking, a large playground, a concession stand, scenic views, and bird-watching.

ACKNOWLEDGMENT: Staff at Iowa Department of Natural Resources

Pine Lake State Park

LOCATION: ½ mile southeast of Eldora on Highway 118 in Hardin County

ADDRESS: Eldora, Iowa 50627

TELEPHONE: (515) 858-5832

HISTORY: In the early 1920s, the citizens of Eldora asked the state to develop an artificial lake and state park here. The Eldora Community Club offered financial assistance in the project. The first 200 acres of the park were acquired by the state in 1921. Located along Pine Creek near its junction with the Iowa River, the park became one of the first state-owned parks. In 1922 the state built a dam across the creek, establishing Pine Lake, the first lake built by the state.

In 1934 an additional 200 acres was acquired. In that same year, four hundred members of the Civilian Conservation Corps worked in developing the park, earning about thirty dollars a month. From 1934 to 1935, they constructed another dam ¼ mile north of Pine Lake. Upper Pine Lake was thus formed with more than 2 miles of shoreline.

DESCRIPTION: Lower Pine Lake covers 50 acres and has a maximum depth of 10 feet. An island is located near the center of the lake. A swimming beach and beach house are located on the northwest shore. The lake also has a boat ramp. Northwest of the lake are Indian mounds. Ringing the lake are hiking and snowmobile trails. The park has a total of 10 miles of hiking trails, including two nature trails.

Upper Pine Lake covers 69 acres and has a concession stand, boat ramp, and campground near the southwest shore. The dam is located on the south shore. Boat rental and boat motor rental are available at the concession stand. Only electric boat motors are permitted on the two lakes.

From 1976 to 1980, a fish restocking was done at Upper Pine Lake, including bluegill, channel catfish, crappie, northern pike, and largemouth

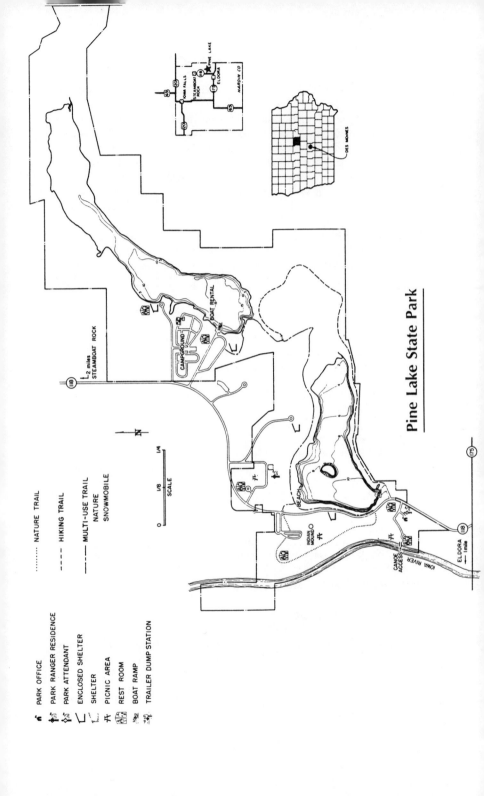

Pine Lake State Park

NATURE TRAIL

- - - - HIKING TRAIL

———— MULTI-USE TRAIL
NATURE
SNOWMOBILE

PARK OFFICE
PARK RANGER RESIDENCE
PARK ATTENDANT
ENCLOSED SHELTER
SHELTER
PICNIC AREA
REST ROOM
BOAT RAMP
TRAILER DUMP STATION

SCALE
0   1/8   1/4

N

CAMPGROUND

BOAT RENTAL

2 miles
STEAMBOAT ROCK

BEACH

INDIAN
MOUND

CANOE ACCESS

IOWA RIVER

ELDORA
1 mile

DES MOINES

PINE LAKE

STEAMBOAT
ROCK

ELDORA

HARDIN CO

bass. Bullheads, catfish, and smallmouth bass are also present. Fishing is also offered on the Iowa River.

Between the lakes are additional hiking and snowmobile trails. There are also two nature trails. The Lakeside Nature Trail is about 1 mile long and runs from the campground at the upper lake to the beach on the lower lake. The Hogsback Nature Trail is about ¾ of a mile in length. It begins at a sandstone bluff, the Hogsback, that overlooks the western side of the lower lake. The trail ends at the beach. A picnic area and shelter are located at the Hogsback. The sandstone is Pennsylvanian in age, probably the Floris Formation.

Covering 572 acres and with a total of seven picnic areas, Pine Lake State Park has become one of Iowa's more popular parks. Hundreds of thousands of visitors come here annually. One of the most popular attractions is the pine-scented air. A few miles to the northwest is the Steamboat Rock Area, state owned but managed by the Hardin County Conservation Board.

FLORA: The lakes were so named because of the abundance of white pine trees, some of which are more than two hundred years old. White birch trees are also present. Along the Iowa River, some rare ferns can be seen.

ACTIVITIES: In 1968 the 128-site campground was moved from the lower lake to the southwest shore of the upper lake. Modern restrooms, showers, and electrical hookups were added. The campground is considered to be among the best in the state and is frequently filled to capacity.

Other activities include swimming, boat ramps, hiking, picnicking, snowmobiling, nature trails, boat rental, boat motor rental, scenic views, and fishing. A sandstone lodge, built by the CCC, overlooks Pine Creek from the north and is available for rental. Historic stone family cabins are being renovated and will be available for rental in 1992.

Finally, adjacent to the park is a nine-hole golf course, the Pine Lake Country Club. It is considered to be one of the most scenic golf courses in the state and has been in use for at least fifty years.

ACKNOWLEDGMENT: Larry Kenyon, park ranger, Pine Lake State Park

FOR MORE INFORMATION:
Pine Lake Edition (annual). Eldora: Hardin County Index.
Pine Lake State Park. Des Moines: Iowa Department of Natural Resources.

Pioneer State Park

LOCATION: 6 miles west and south of Riceville on Highway 9, then 1 mile west on County Road T-54, in Mitchell County

ADDRESS: Mitchell County Conservation Board, Osage, Iowa 50461

TELEPHONE: (515) 732-5204 (Mitchell County Conservation Board)

HISTORY: In 1933 the Little Cedar Valley Conservation Club was organized by citizens from the Little Cedar–Brownville area. Their purpose was to acquire land in Mitchell County to develop public parks. Their first project involved acquiring land along the Little Cedar River west of Brownville with the intention of developing it into a state park. Ten acres were acquired from Angelia Byrnes, Kathryn Erwin, George Nelson, and Louis Sanders. Through the 1930s, they developed the park, which included a 25-acre pond that had been used for an old mill.

In 1938 the park was turned over to the state, and the club disbanded. The Pioneer State Park, named to honor the early settlers in Mitchell County, was opened on July 7, 1938, and officially dedicated on August 7, 1938. Several thousand people attended the dedication. A six-ton glacier boulder was hauled to the southeast entrance of the park, and a dedication plaque was mounted on it. Two millstones originally from France were placed on either side of the boulder. Before the ceremony, pine trees were planted around the dedication site.

In 1939 a shelter was built from glacial stones found nearby. The building and its fireplace were constructed by Anferd Olson, a stone mason from Adams, Minnesota. Anferd was seventy-three at the time and received three dollars a day. Local citizens assisted in the construction.

ACTIVITIES: Today Pioneer State Park covers 18 acres and offers camping, picnicking, and fishing in the Little Cedar River.

ACKNOWLEDGMENT: Staff at Mitchell County Conservation Board, Osage, Iowa

Pleasant Creek State Recreation Area

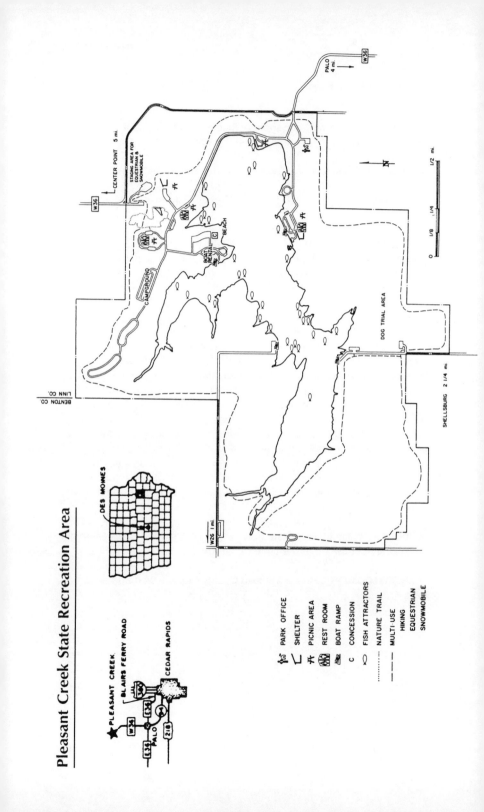

DES MOINES

★ PLEASANT CREEK
BLAIRS FERRY ROAD
W 36
PALO
E 34
210
CEDAR RAPIDS

LINN CO.
BENTON CO.

W36 ← CENTER POINT 5 mi.

STAGING AREA FOR EQUESTRIAN & SNOWMOBILE

W36
PALO 4 mi.

CAMPGROUND

BEACH

BOAT RENTAL

DOG TRIAL AREA

SHELLSBURG 2 1/4 mi.

W26 1 mi.

N

0   1/8   1/4   1/2 mi.

PARK OFFICE
SHELTER
PICNIC AREA
REST ROOM
BOAT RAMP
C   CONCESSION
FISH ATTRACTORS
NATURE TRAIL
MULTI-USE
    HIKING
    EQUESTRIAN
    SNOWMOBILE

Pleasant Creek State Recreation Area

LOCATION: 4 miles north and ½ mile west of Palo on County Road W-36 in Linn County

ADDRESS: Drawer C, Palo, Iowa 52324

TELEPHONE: (319) 436-7716

HISTORY: In the 1960s, the Iowa Conservation Commission began searching for a place to be used as a recreation area serving the Waterloo, Cedar Rapids, and Iowa City areas, which have a combined population of more than 600,000. Meanwhile, the Iowa Electric Light and Power Company needed a reservoir to provide backup cooling water for the Duane Arnold Atomic Energy Center located to the south. Water from the Cedar River is used for plant cooling, but during dry spells, water is sometimes needed to supplement flows in the Cedar River. Both organizations decided to work together on an artificial lake in the Pleasant Creek area. Work on the lake began in the 1970s, and the lake was filled to capacity by 1978.

DESCRIPTION: Covering 1,927 acres, Pleasant Creek became the first completed state recreation area in Iowa. State recreation areas are normally open all year, twenty-four hours a day, and offer the widest possible variety of outdoor activities. An estimated 220,000 visitors come here annually.

Covering 410 acres, the lake has a maximum depth of 60 feet near the dam. Jetties were constructed along the shore and extend up to 300 feet into the lake, providing excellent shore fishing. Rough fish were killed off by chemicals, and channel catfish, largemouth bass, bluegill, crappie, and tiger muskie were stocked.

A supervised swimming area is located on the north shore to the west of the dam. Also in that area are a boat ramp and a concession stand offering fishing supplies, refreshments, and boat rental. Any size boat motors may be used at no-wake speeds. Three other boat ramps are present around the lake. Picnic areas with shelters are located on the northeast and southeast shores. These are available for reservation. A nature trail can be found on the north end. The dam offers a scenic view of the recreation area, which is a combination of wooded hills, marshy areas, and meadows.

ACTIVITIES: A campground is present with electricity, modern showers, and restroom facilities. There are numerous trails for hiking, bicycling, snowmobiling, and horseback riding. In all, 15 miles of trails have been established.

Other activities include cross-country skiing, sledding, ice-skating, a large playground structure, hunting, swimming, boat rental, fishing, picnicking, a nature trail, and scenic views.

ACKNOWLEDGMENT: Randy R. Edwards, park ranger, Pleasant Creek State Recreation Area

FOR MORE INFORMATION:
   Pleasant Creek State Recreation Area. Des Moines: Iowa Department of Natural Resources.

Steamboat Rock Area

LOCATION: Southern edge of Steamboat Rock, less than a mile west of Highway 118 on a county road, in Hardin County

ADDRESS: Hardin County Conservation Board, Ackley, Iowa 50601

TELEPHONE: (515) 858-3461 (Hardin County Conservation Board)

HISTORY: The town of Steamboat Rock (originally Lithopolis) was founded in 1855 and was the first town in the county. The first resident was Sanford Baldwin.
   In 1856 Samuel Higgenbotham, Isaac Lesh, and Charles Boyle built a dam and sawmill on the river here. The next year, S. F. Lathrop acquired the property and built a three-story gristmill costing ten thousand dollars. The mill burned in 1910. Later, the Central States Power and Light Company in Cedar Rapids used the old dam. The original Steamboat Rock State Park was a 4-acre area near the dam and was purchased from the power company in the 1920s. A shelter was built in 1938, and in that same year, a new dam was built.

DESCRIPTION: The area's name and the name of the town both came from a bluff that rises up to 60 feet above the river. The bluff—comprising brown sandstone of the Pennsylvanian Period, probably the Floris Formation—resembled a steamboat, according to early settlers. Erosion has altered the shape of the bluff, and it was struck by lightning in 1858. Nearby is another bluff, Tower Rock, which rises to 90 feet above the river. The Hardin County Conservation Board manages a number of areas that comprise the "Iowa River Greenbelt." One of these is the Steamboat Rock Area.

About 2 miles to the southeast is Pine Lake State Park.

ACTIVITIES: Steamboat Rock Area is a 5-acre site offering camping, scenic views, and boating and fishing in the Iowa River. Some unusual plant life can be found here.

ACKNOWLEDGMENT: Staff at Eldora Public Library, Eldora, Iowa

Turkey River Mounds State Preserve

LOCATION: About ½ mile north of Millville on Highway 52, turn east on a gravel road and continue for about 2 miles to the preserve.

DESCRIPTION: The preserve was an Indian burial ground around two thousand years ago, with forty-six burial mounds being present. Today, the Turkey River Mounds is an archaeological preserve of 62 acres overlooking the confluence of the Turkey and Mississippi rivers. A forested ridge of dolomitic limestone of the Ordovician Period, Dunleith and Wise Lake formations, has been eroded into scenic pinnacles. The ridge rises up to 200 feet above the Turkey River and is ¾ of a mile in length with a deep valley on both sides.

The preserve was officially dedicated on September 23, 1968, and lies along the Mississippi River floodplain. There are forested islands in the river comprising part of the Upper Mississippi River National Wildlife Refuge.

FLORA: Present in the preserve is a wide variety of plants, including trees, shrubs, ferns, and wildflowers.

Union Grove State Park

LOCATION: 4 miles southwest of Gladbrook off County Road T-47 in Tama County

ADDRESS: Gladbrook, Iowa 50635

TELEPHONE: (515) 473-2556

HISTORY: The town of Union Grove was founded here in the early 1850s. However, when the railroad bypassed the community, Union Grove began to decline. Its residents united with the residents of Badger Hill, located 6 miles to the north, and founded the town of Gladbrook. The old town site of Union Grove is located on the floor of the present artificial lake.

In 1935 the Tama County board of supervisors selected this site for a future state park and lake. Although federal funding was available for park development through the Works Progress Administration (WPA) there were no funds for the purchase of land. In response, local citizens formed the Lake Park and Holding Corp., Inc., a nonprofit organization. They raised an initial $35,900.

In 1936 the WPA began work on the dam, spillway, lake, and park. Forty-five thousand dollars was provided by the government, and $50,000 was provided by the Lake Park and Holding Corp. In 1940 the park was sold to the state for $10,000.

DESCRIPTION: Union Grove State Park comprises 282 acres and has a 118-acre artificial lake. In later years, a siltation problem was noticed in the lake, and the problem has become worse, cutting the lake's depth in half in some places. The depth was originally 35 feet. A lake-reclamation plan involving state, county, and local agencies was developed. Conservation-minded farming practices are being implemented in the 6,600-acre watershed, and the lake was dredged between 1988 and 1990. An aeration system will be installed to prevent winter fish kills.

ACTIVITIES: A 32-site campground with electricity and nonmodern restrooms is present. Hiking, unsupervised swimming, picnicking, fishing, snowmobiling, boat ramps (any size motors may be used at no-wake speeds), and boat rental are also offered.

ACKNOWLEDGMENT: Wesley Jones, park ranger, Union Grove State Park

Volga River State Recreation Area

LOCATION: 4 miles north of Fayette off Highway 150 in Fayette County

ADDRESS: Fayette, Iowa 52142

TELEPHONE: (319) 425-4161

HISTORY: The Volga River State Recreation Area comprises more than 5,400 acres acquired in the 1960s and 1970s, including the Big Rock Wildlife Management Area. Construction of the 135-acre Frog Hollow Lake was done between 1978 and 1979. Concrete culverts, old tires, and other structures were placed on the previously featureless lakebed to provide shelters for fish.

DESCRIPTION: The recreation area has densely wooded timber, prairies with wildlife food and cover plantings, sinkholes, caves, and limestone bluffs of the Maquoketa Formation, Ordovician Period. The Volga River meanders for 7 miles through the southern area of the park. Frog Hollow Creek flows from the lake in the northern edge of the park and joins the river in the central area.

There are 17 miles of hiking and equestrian trails, and visitors can obtain a map and trail guides from the ranger. Trails include Frog Hollow Trail, Lake View Trail, Ridge Trail, Albany Trail, and the Lima Trail. The Lima Trail takes visitors past 20-foot-high limestone bluffs and a 15-acre white pine plantation. The Albany Trail includes the Albany Bridge, an old steel bridge over the river.

FLORA AND FAUNA: Many species of mammals are present, and there is abundant bird life, including ducks, shorebirds, songbirds, hawks, and owls. Aspen and Canadian yew trees are common.

ACTIVITIES: There is a 32-site campground lacking electricity, modern restrooms, or showers. Cross-country skiing, bridle trails, hiking trails, and a boat ramp are also offered. Any size boat motors may be used on the lake but at no-wake speeds. For fishermen, the lake offers bluegill, largemouth bass, and channel catfish, among others. The Volga River has smallmouth bass, rock bass, channel catfish, and white suckers. Canoeing on the river has become popular.

In the winter, some trails are maintained for snowmobiling. Snowmobilers are asked to remain on the groomed trails. They should get a report on trail conditions from the ranger beforehand. Snowmobilers are also asked to use the parking area at the lake as a staging area.

Hunting for deer, wild turkey, grouse, squirrel, and rabbit is very popular. Hunter-access parking areas are located in the eastern and southern parts.

ACKNOWLEDGMENT: Jerry Reisinger, park ranger, Volga River State Recreation Area

FOR MORE INFORMATION:
   Trail Guide: Volga River State Recreation Area. Des Moines: Iowa Department of Natural Resources.
   Volga River State Recreation Area. Des Moines: Iowa Department of Natural Resources.

Wapsipinicon State Park

LOCATION: Southern edge of Anamosa along Highway 151 in Jones County

ADDRESS: R.R. 2, Anamosa, Iowa 52205

TELEPHONE: (319) 462-2761

HISTORY: In February of 1921, citizens in the Anamosa area held a meeting to consider purchasing land for a state park. In only a few weeks time, they had raised $20,000. They purchased 183 acres from Asa W. Smith for $22,936. In April of that same year, the land was donated to the state and became one of the first donated state parks. Early development was done by prisoners from the Men's Reformatory in Anamosa during a five-year period. One of the projects involved blasting through some of the bluffs. Local students were let out of school to watch the blasting. Blasting at Horse Thief Cave uncovered at least nine human skeletons, animal bones, artifacts, and pottery believed to be around four thousand years old (Archaic Culture).
   The name Wapsipinicon is a combination of two Indian names. Wapsi was a Fox squaw. Pinnekon was a Sac brave. The two were lovers who were eventually wedded.

DESCRIPTION: Today the park covers 251 acres along the Wapsipinicon River and has several caves. Horse Thief Cave is said to have been a hideout for horse thieves. Another cave, Ice Cave, remains cool whatever the outside temperature.

A nine-hole golf course is located in the eastern part of the park. It is maintained by the Anamosa Country Club. An enclosed lodge in the north central part is open to the public on a rental basis. The western area offers a scenic view and an interpretive trail. Dutch Creek winds through the southern part of the park, which also includes snowmobile trails and the caves. Hiking trails can be found throughout the park. There are bluffs of dolomitic limestone in the park that are part of the Scotch Grove Formation, Silurian Period.

FLORA AND FAUNA: The park has a large variety of plant and animal life. The oldest white pine planting in Iowa can be found here. Wildflowers include jack-in-the-pulpit, Mayapple, and bellwort. Moss and columbine hang over the cave entrances. Wildlife include black squirrels, fox squirrels, gray squirrels, beavers, and deer.

ACTIVITIES: The park offers picnicking, hiking, a rental lodge, fishing, snowmobiling, mushroom hunting, nature study, caves, an interpretive trail, scenic views, golfing, and a thirty-site campground located in the center of the park that has modern restrooms, showers, and fifteen electrically equipped sites.

Fishing can be done in the Wapsipinicon River, and there are no restrictions on the size of boat motors. A modern boat ramp provides excellent boating access. Channel catfish, flathead catfish, bullheads, crappies, northern pike, largemouth bass, and walleyes are present. Fishing can also be done at the mouth of Dutch Creek when the water level is high.

ACKNOWLEDGMENT: Park ranger, Wapsipinicon State Park

FOR MORE INFORMATION:
Wapsipinicon State Park. Des Moines: Iowa Department of Natural Resources.

Yellow River State Forest

LOCATION: 14 miles southeast of Waukon on Highway 76 in Allamakee County

ADDRESS: Area Forester, P.O. Box 115, McGregor, Iowa 52157

TELEPHONE: (319) 586-2548

HISTORY: An Indian school was opened in this area in 1835. Soldiers from Fort Crawford, Wisconsin, under the command of Zachary Taylor and Lieutenant Jefferson Davis assisted in its construction. The school was closed in 1840. Later, Taylor vacationed here with his family, as did Andrew Jackson. The school's old foundation is still present in the forest.

The state acquired the land in the 1930s. At that time, 1,500 acres along the Yellow River were included. This portion later became the Effigy Mounds National Monument and belongs to the National Park Service.

DESCRIPTION: The forest is composed of seven units. These are:

• Paint Creek Unit covers 3,357 acres and is the main part of the forest. Located 3 miles southwest of Waterville, the unit has been well developed for public use.

• Lost Forty Unit covers 160 acres and is located 2 miles north and 3½ miles west of McGregor. It is maintained as a watershed and forest management area.

• Luster Heights Unit covers 651 acres and is located 1 mile south of Waukon Junction. It is used as a forest management area and a Social Services camp.

• Mudhen Unit covers 196 acres along the Mississippi River east of Waukon Junction. It is a bottomland forest on the Mississippi River floodplain.

• Paint Rock Unit covers 714 acres and is located 2 miles southwest of Harpers Ferry. It is an undeveloped area adjacent to the Mississippi River.

• Waukon Junction Unit covers 298 acres on the northern edge of Waukon Junction adjacent to the Mississippi River.

• Yellow River Unit covers 192 acres of upland and bottomland forest and watershed area. It is located 4 miles north and 3 miles west of McGregor.

In the vicinity of, and included in, the forest are exposures of limestone of the Decorah and Platteville formations and sandstone of the Saint Peter Formation, all of the Ordovician Period.

In the Paint Creek Unit are several marked and unmarked hiking trails. These include:

• Backpack Trail begins at the information area adjacent to the forest headquarters. Covering a total of 20 miles, the trail has been split into five sections to allow shorter trips if desired. Along the trail, people can see numerous oak, hickory, and walnut trees. A dense growth of young walnuts can be seen in the vicinity of Brown's Hollow, located in the south central area of the unit. A spring is present on the southern end of the hollow.

• Evergreen Trail begins at the fire tower. The tower, located in the center of the unit, was the first of its kind in Iowa. It is not open for public viewing. The trail is a leisurely one of about an hour in length and offers many species of evergreen trees, which are identified by signs.

• Bluff Trail joins the Backpack Trail. It begins at the junction of the abandoned railroad track and the Waterville access road (northwest of the main access road). This is located north of the bridge over Paint Creek. The trail is steep in places and somewhat tiring. Two scenic views are offered. The east one provides a view of the forest headquarters, a sawmill operated by the Department of Natural Resources, and southern areas of the unit. The Cherry Mound Church can be seen near the headquarters. The west overlook provides a view of the campground, Paint Creek, and several plantations of pine trees. Along the trail are numerous trees identified by signs. The trail requires less than an hour of walking.

• Research Trail is used by Iowa State University, the U.S. Forest Service, and the Department of Natural Resources. The trail requires about an hour of hiking and leads past areas where research has been conducted, such as studies on tree growth and the long-term effects of herbicides on white pine trees.

In 1973 a memorial plaque was placed in the forest honoring Manford A. Ellerhoff (1910–71). He was a former district forester for the Conservation Commission and a strong supporter of the development of the Yellow River State Forest.

The forest also includes two marshes and more than fifty small ponds.

ACTIVITIES: Totaling 5,568 acres, the forest has become the most popular of Iowa's state forests and is the most developed. The majority of the facilities are located in the Paint Creek Unit. Inside the unit are two trout streams, Big Paint Creek, and Little Paint Creek. The unit offers picnic grounds, scenic views, nature study, snowmobile trails, hiking trails, bridle trails, cross-country skiing, camping, and hunting. There is a total of 176 campsites. Electricity, modern restrooms, and showers are not available.

Water is available only at the forest headquarters located just inside the main entrance on the western edge of the Paint Creek Unit. There are other entrances to the forest. Hunting for deer, squirrel, grouse, turkey, rabbit, and woodcock are permitted.

ACKNOWLEDGMENT: John McSweeny, area forester, Yellow River State Forest

FOR MORE INFORMATION:

Yellow River Forest. Des Moines: Iowa Department of Natural Resources.

Yellow River State Forest Backpacking Trails. Des Moines: Iowa Department of Natural Resources.

View from a cave overlooking the river at Starrs Cave Park and Preserve.

2 Southeast Iowa

Flint Creek runs through Starrs Cave Park and Preserve.

Devil's Punch Bowl at Wildcat Den State Park.

Pine Creek gristmill at Wildcat Den State Park.

Bobwhite State Park

LOCATION: 1 mile west of Allerton on County Road J-46 in Wayne County

ADDRESS: Allerton, Iowa 50008

TELEPHONE: (515) 873-4670

HISTORY: Back in 1846, an estimated five hundred covered wagons camped here on their trek westward, following the "Mormon Trail."
In the early 1930s, the Rock Island Railroad built a reservoir here to provide water for their steam engines. In 1947 the state purchased the body of water and surrounding land from the Chicago, Rock Island, and Pacific Railway Company, and from the Saint Paul and Kansas City Short Line Railroad Company.

DESCRIPTION: Located on the Mormon Pioneer National Historic Trail, Bobwhite State Park was named after the bobwhite quail, whose call can be heard early in the morning. It covers 390 acres and has an artificial lake of 89 acres.

FLORA: The staff at the park is particularly proud of their fine nature trail. The "My Native Land Nature Trail" requires one hour of walking. It is a well-maintained and level trail, along which visitors can see abundant wildflowers, timber, and native prairie grasses.

ACTIVITIES: There is a 32-site campground with electricity but with non-modern restroom facilities. A nature trail, picnicking, unsupervised swimming, fishing, and boating (electric motors only) are offered. Mushroom hunting and berry picking are permitted. The park is also popular with bird-watchers. A shelter was built on a hill overlooking the lake and is available for reservation.

ACKNOWLEDGMENTS: Keith Allen, park ranger, and Lorena Blount, Bobwhite State Park

FOR MORE INFORMATION:
Bobwhite Nature Trail. Des Moines: Iowa Department of Natural Resources.
National Park Service, U.S. Department of the Interior. *Mormon Pioneer National Historic Trail.* Washington, D.C.: Government Printing Office, 1981.

Elk Rock State Park

LOCATION: 7 miles north of Knoxville off Highway 14 in Marion County

ADDRESS: R.R. 1, Box 45, Otley, Iowa 50214

TELEPHONE: (515) 627-5434

HISTORY: The site of the present-day Red Rock Lake has been inhabited by Indians dating back more than five thousand years to the Archaic Culture. Evidence of habitation during the later Woodland and Oneota cultures has also been found. The Oneota Indians were probably the ancestors of the Ioway Indians. In 1842, the Sac and Fox Indians granted settlers the right to this land. The Indians called the area Sic-ella-musk-achees or "place of the red stones." Chief Keokuk, subchief Kish-ke-kosh, and other leaders welcomed the settlers and treated them well.

In 1960 the U.S. Army Corps of Engineers began work on a dam located 6 miles southwest of Pella. This was part of a flood-control project on the Des Moines River. Total cost of the Red Rock project was eighty-eight million dollars. It took nine years to complete the 1½-mile-long dam, which supports a highway.

In 1969 the Corps of Engineers leased land along the reservoir, northeast of the Highway 14 bridge, to the state. The land became known as Elk Rock State Park. Elk Rock was known to early settlers as an unusual rock feature near this site.

In 1978 the state obtained a lease for property on the south shore of the reservoir, southeast of the bridge. This area is called South Elk Rock.

DESCRIPTION: The average size of Red Rock Lake is around 10,000 acres, but during times of heavy rains, it has a maximum capacity of 65,000 acres. When flooding occurs, the silt is deposited in the western part of the reservoir. The eastern part remains clear.

Above the water level at the northern end of the reservoir, portions of the red sandstone bluffs of old quarries are still visible. The bluffs represent the Pennsylvania period, Floris formation.

The Highway 14 bridge crosses the western part of the reservoir. At 5,460 feet in length, this is the longest bridge in the state.

North Elk Rock has seven picnic areas, eight shelters available on a first-come basis, modern restrooms, trails, and a three-lane boat ramp.

The day-use area of South Elk Rock has two picnic grounds, shelters, modern restrooms, and a trail access to the lake. The main portion has a two-lane boat ramp and a 40-site campground with modern restrooms and showers and 12 electrical sites. A new equestrian campground is available for horseback riding enthusiasts. This 33-site campground has 24 electrical sites, a shower building, and three sun shelters for horses. An excellent system of horseback trails radiates outward from the campground.

In addition to Elk Rock State Park, there are several other public areas around the reservoir, managed by the Marion County Conservation Board, the U.S. Army Corps of Engineers, and the Department of Natural Resources. More than a million people visit the Red Rock area annually.

FLORA AND FAUNA: The reservoir area has abundant flora and fauna, including more than 200 species of birds, 54 species of trees, 62 species of wildflowers, 43 species of fish, and 35 species of mammals.

Ten thousand acres have been set aside in two areas along the Des Moines River northwest of the reservoir. They serve as a refuge for migrating waterfowl. Hunting in these areas is prohibited. They are open to the public except during the autumn migration period (mid-September to mid-December). Thousands of geese and ducks migrate through here, including Canadian geese, blue geese, snow geese, and white-fronted geese. Occasionally, bald eagles and double-crested cormorants can be seen. Because of the great variety in birds, this area has become popular with bird-watchers.

ACTIVITIES: The combined area of Elk Rock State Park comprises 2,218 acres of wooded hills offering camping, hiking, a nature trail, bridle trails, scenic overlooks, fishing (catfish, crappie, and white bass, especially), snowmobiling, and boating. There is no limit on horsepower for boat motors. Boaters and water-skiers need to use caution, however, especially during high winds. A yellow light on the dam warns people on the water of winds in the 10–25 MPH range. A red light means stronger winds. During times of high water, the boat ramps at Elk Rock are not usable. In addition, high winds can clog the ramps with debris, not only at Elk Rock but at the water station on the south shore and the marina bay on the north shore as well. When the water level is high, the western areas of the reservoir can hide submerged obstacles such as trees, roads, and fence posts. It is not advisable to leave boats on the shore overnight because the water level can fluctuate widely. Information on boating conditions can be obtained from the Department of Natural Resources' Lake Red Rock water station, telephone: (515) 842–3805. Camping, fishing, and boating information can be obtained from the U.S. Army Corps of Engineers, telephone: (800) 362–2001.

In addition to the above activities, hunting is also allowed in the 25,000-acre Red Rock Wildlife Management Area. Waterfowl, pheasant, quail, deer, rabbit, and squirrel can be hunted.

ACKNOWLEDGMENT: Gary Galliart, park ranger, Elk Rock State Park

FOR MORE INFORMATION:

Elk Rock State Park. Des Moines: Iowa Department of Natural Resources.

U.S. Army Corps of Engineers, Department of Defense. *Lake Red Rock.* Washington, D.C.: Government Printing Office.

Fairport Station Recreation Area

LOCATION: 5 miles east of Muscatine on Highway 22 in Muscatine County

ADDRESS: Wildcat Den State Park, R.R. 3, Box 170, Muscatine, Iowa 52761

TELEPHONE: (319) 263-3197

HISTORY: Located near the recreation area is the Fairport Fish Management Unit. The first research station was started here by the U.S. Fish Commission in 1908. Called the Fairport Biological Station, the center was first used for research on mussels in the Mississippi River. The station grew to become the top fisheries center in the nation. Research expanded to include channel catfish, largemouth bass, buffalo fish, paddlefish, sturgeon, and turtles. Before its decline in the 1920s, the center had grown to 60 acres, with several living quarters and a three-story research laboratory. Lack of interest and funds caused the center's decline, as new centers opened up on the Pacific Coast. The building was demolished in 1972.

In 1973 the state acquired the land and used it as a hatchery for largemouth bass and bluegills. Later they also began raising grass carp, which are useful in controlling vegetation growth in lakes. In 1975 the Conservation Commission's Fairport Fish Management Unit was developed to study fish and fish habitats in the Mississippi River.

DESCRIPTION: Fairport Station Recreation Area is a "satellite" of Wildcat Den State Park, which is located 6 miles to the east along Highway 22. Fairport is basically a campground with two boat ramps on the Mississippi River. It comprises 17 acres. The campground has 43 sites. Electricity is available as well as modern restrooms and shower facilities.

ACTIVITIES: Camping, fishing, and boat docks are available. In the Mississippi River, channel catfish, crappie, sauger, bluegill, white bass, and wall-eye can be caught.

ACKNOWLEDGMENT: Beverly Reasoner, park attendant, Wildcat Den State Park

Galland School

LOCATION: 3 miles south of Montrose on County Road X-28 in Lee County

HISTORY: In 1829 Dr. Isaac Galland, a botanist, and his family settled in a clearing near an area of rapids on the Mississippi River. In 1830 he built a 10-by-12-foot log schoolhouse, the first in the state. The first two students were his son and the son of another settler. The teacher, Berryman Jennings, received a salary of room and board and the use of the professor's library. At one time, up to eighteen students were enrolled, and a community of about a dozen families grew here. Several of the students were from Illinois.

The school closed in 1833, and the building was later demolished for the wood, which was used in heating surrounding cabins.

In 1913 a dam was built at Keokuk on the Mississippi River, and the resulting high water flooded the site of the old school located upriver.

DESCRIPTION: The present Galland School is a replica built in 1940 and dedicated in October of that year. The building is located several hundred feet west of the original site. Construction was done by the Lee County Schoolmasters Club. Funding was provided by several local organizations, schools, and individuals.

The site occupies about ½ acre of land.

ACKNOWLEDGMENT: Staff at the State Archives

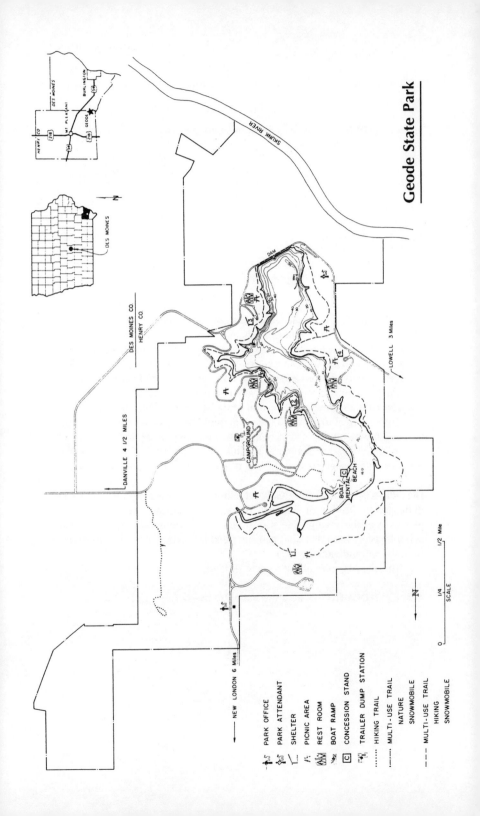

Geode State Park

Geode State Park

LOCATION: 10 miles west of Burlington on Highway 34, and then on Highway 79, in Henry County

ADDRESS: R.R. 1, Danville, Iowa 52623

TELEPHONE: (319) 392-4601

HISTORY: Although Geode State Park had its start back in the 1930s when the state purchased the land from Charlie Hall and the Civilian Conservation Corps first developed it, most of the development in the park was done after World War II. Up until 1968, prisoners from Fort Madison periodically worked to improve the park's facilities.

In 1950 a dam was built to form Lake Geode, with a deep shoreline ringed with timber. At first, fishing was good in the 300-acre lake with a maximum depth of 50 feet at the dam. However, several problems caused sporadic fishing in later years. These included siltation, inclement weather, and predation or the killing of smaller fish by larger fish. In 1981 the lake was drained and renovated.

DESCRIPTION: When dedicated on June 20, 1951, Geode State Park comprised 600 acres. Today the park comprises 1,640 acres and receives hundreds of thousands of visitors annually. The campground has become very popular.

The 200-unit campground is located in the eastern part of the park. Eighty electrical hookups are available, and modern restrooms and showers are present. Displayed at the campground are some geodes, Iowa's state rock. Although collecting within the park is prohibited, geodes have been found in many places in the surrounding area. Within the park and the vicinity are exposures of several Mississippian-Period formations: Burlington, Keokuk, Warsaw, St. Louis, and Spergen.

Picnic areas are located on the north, east, south, and southwest shores of the lake, and they are all connected by trails. The park has 4½ miles of hiking trails. The main trail runs from the north end of the lake to the dam on the south end. There are four shelters available, which may be reserved. A large playground structure is provided for children.

The Skunk River forms the southern boundary of the park. A small cemetery in this area has grave markers dating from the 1820s to the 1850s. A nature trail used by the Boy Scouts, the Sho-quo-quon Trail, begins at the dam and leads south through part of the park to the river. It runs parallel to the Skunk River for a while, then leads east to Burlington, a distance of 20 miles.

63

Lake Geode has nearly 6 miles of shoreline, including a 300-foot-wide beach on the north shore. The lake has largemouth bass, bluegills, crappies, channel catfish, bullheads, sunfish, and tiger muskies. Any size boat motors may be operated at no-wake speeds.

FLORA AND FAUNA: Much of the park remains in a beautiful, natural state. Present are many wildflowers and trees.

ACTIVITIES: The beach is a great place to swim or sun yourself. The concession stand is open from mid-April to mid-September. There are lifeguards at the beach during the summer, and a small fee is charged to use the beach and bathhouse. Boats are available for rent, and fishing supplies are available. Other activities offered at the park include snowmobiling, cross-country skiing, sailboating, hiking, fishing, picnicking, a nature trail, and especially, camping.

ACKNOWLEDGMENT: Gary Fell, park ranger, Geode State Park

FOR MORE INFORMATION:
Geode State Park. Des Moines: Iowa Department of Natural Resources.

Honey Creek State Park

LOCATION: 9½ miles west of Moravia on Highway 142, then 3½ miles southeast on a county road, in Appanoose County

ADDRESS: R.R. 2, Moravia, Iowa 52571

TELEPHONE: (515) 724-3739

HISTORY: Since the dam was completed on the Chariton River by the U.S. Army Corps of Engineers and the gates closed in October of 1969, the Rathbun Lake has become a very popular recreation area. By 1970 the 1,000-acre lake was full, creating 160 miles of shoreline.

DESCRIPTION: The 828-acre Honey Creek State Park is located on a peninsula on the northeastern part of the lake's north shore. The campground is located in the central area of the park. An unsupervised beach for swim-

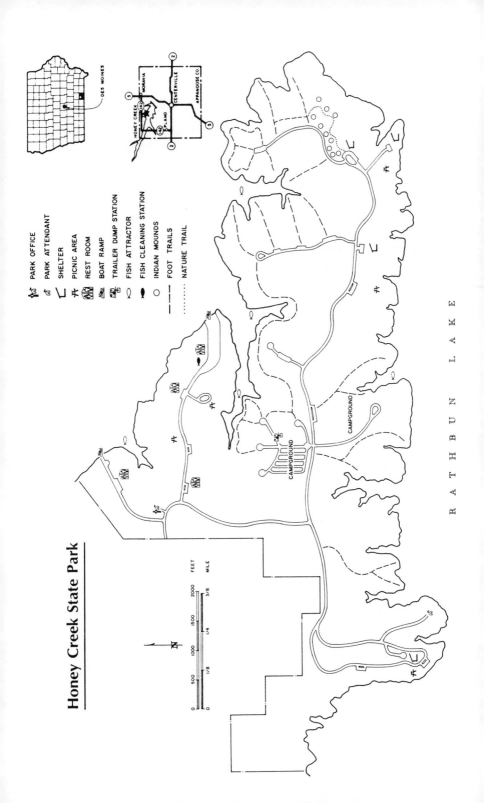

Honey Creek State Park

DES MOINES

MORAVIA
CENTERVILLE
APPANOOSE CO
HONEY CREEK
PLANO

PARK OFFICE
PARK ATTENDANT
SHELTER
PICNIC AREA
REST ROOM
BOAT RAMP
TRAILER DUMP STATION
FISH ATTRACTOR
FISH CLEANING STATION
INDIAN MOUNDS
FOOT TRAILS
NATURE TRAIL

N

FEET
MILE

0   500   1000   1500   2000
0   1/8   1/4   3/8

CAMPGROUND
CAMPGROUND
CAMPGROUND

R A T H B U N   L A K E

mers is located in the north central part. Two boat ramps are found in Honey Creek. In the eastern area are Indian mounds.

A state fish hatchery was opened in the area in 1978. Covering 375 acres, it is located just below the dam. Included is an office building, twenty rearing ponds, pollution-control ponds, a visitor center, and an observation walkway. Visitors can view the rearing ponds, aquariums, and a fish pond. The hatchery has restrooms. There is also a nature trail for the public. The hatchery was built for warm-water fish, primarily channel catfish. In 1978 over 1 million catfish were raised here. Other fish raised here include walleye, largemouth bass, and striped bass. Hatchery staff also do research on fish diseases and their prevention. The hatchery cost six million dollars and is considered to be among the best in the nation.

Rathbun Lake is the largest body of water in the state. The dam is located in the southwest corner. There are several federal recreation areas in the vicinity, including twelve boat ramps and several campgrounds. More information on these areas is available from the U.S. Army Corps of Engineers.

ACTIVITIES: The lake was the scene of extensive fish stocking in the 1970s. Crappies were the first to be stocked, and they make up the vast majority of the fish caught. Other fish stocked here include walleye, largemouth bass, channel catfish, white bass, muskie, striped bass, and tiger muskie. Spottail shiners were stocked to serve as forage fish. Bluegills, sheepheads, and black bullheads were present in the Chariton River before the lake was constructed. Fishermen can check with the staff of the state fish hatchery for current information on "hot spots."

The park has a newly expanded 167-site campground with modern restrooms and shower facilities. Ninety-two of the sites have electrical hookups. Also offered in the park are picnicking, hiking, scenic views, and snowmobiling. There are three shelters in the park and a self-guided nature trail.

The nearby Rathbun Wildlife Unit offers hunting for waterfowl, quail, deer, pheasant, squirrel, rabbit, and turkey. Public hunting areas are located along the Chariton River to the northwest of the lake and along the South Fork of the Chariton River to the southwest of the lake.

ACKNOWLEDGMENT: Brent Laning, park attendant, Honey Creek State Park

FOR MORE INFORMATION:
Honey Creek State Park. Des Moines: Iowa Department of Natural Resources.

Lacey-Keosauqua State Park

LOCATION: South edge of Keosauqua, immediately south of the Des Moines River, west side of Highway 1, in Van Buren County

ADDRESS: P.O. Box 398, Keosauqua, Iowa 52565

TELEPHONE: (319) 293-3502

HISTORY: The site of present-day Lacey-Keosauqua State Park was a popular area with Sac and Fox Indians before the settlers arrived in the late 1830s. Earlier, Indians of the Woodland Culture are believed to have established a village southwest of "Ely's Ford." At least nineteen of their burial mounds are present there. Keosauqua is an Indian name roughly meaning "the stream with the floating ice."

The town of Keosauqua was founded in 1839, and some of the early settlers were lumberjacks who made their livelihood from timber in the area. Remnants of their cabins may still be found in the park.

In the 1840s, thousands of Mormons passed through the area on their journey west. The original Mormon Trail was located about ½ mile south of the park. A rocky stretch on the river, Ely's Ford, was heavily used as a crossing by the Mormons and others before bridges were built. A sign has been placed at the ford.

In the 1830s and 1840s, the Keosauqua area was the scene of a series of conflicts known as the Honey War. The states of Iowa and Missouri both laid claim to the land. Honey was a prized commodity back when sugar was scarce, and early settlers extracted quite a bit of the natural sweetener from numerous beehives in the local trees. Missouri officials tried to collect taxes on the honey, but the residents refused to pay. Someone then cut down some of the trees, and local lawmen were called in. However, the dispute grew, and the two states threatened each other with their militias. The Clark County court in Missouri took up the case but referred it to Congress, which in turn referred it to the Supreme Court. In 1849 the Supreme Court ruled that the land belonged to Iowa. A plaque commemorating the peaceful settlement was placed in the park's lodge.

In 1919, 160 acres of an area known as "Big Bend" was donated to the state for development as a state park. The area was so named because the Des Moines River makes a wide bend here. An additional 1,062 acres was later added, and Lacey-Keosauqua was officially dedicated as Iowa's second state park on October 27, 1921. On August 15, 1926, an inscription honoring John Fletcher Lacey was placed on a glacial boulder overlooking Ely's Ford. Lacey was a Civil War veteran, a senator, and an early supporter of conservation.

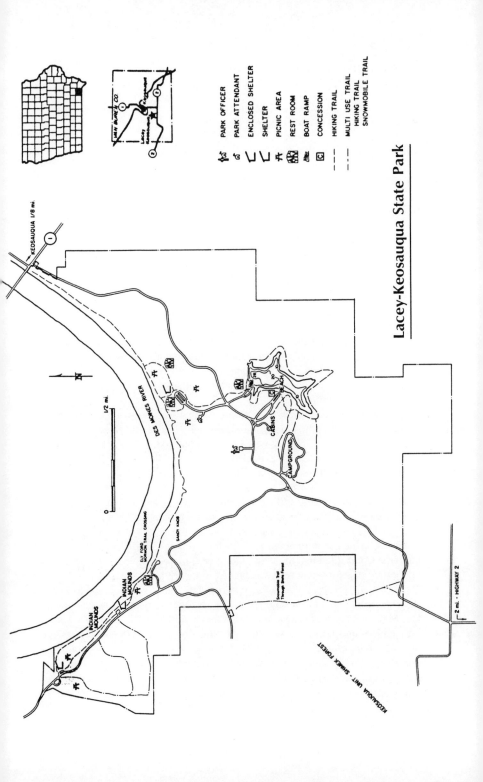

Lacey-Keosauqua State Park

PARK OFFICER
PARK ATTENDANT
ENCLOSED SHELTER
SHELTER
PICNIC AREA
REST ROOM
BOAT RAMP
CONCESSION
HIKING TRAIL
MULTI USE TRAIL
HIKING TRAIL
SNOWMOBILE TRAIL

VAN BUREN CO.

Keosauqua

Lacey-Keosauqua

KEOSAUQUA 1/8 mi.

DES MOINES RIVER

1/2 mi.

N

INDIAN MOUNDS
INDIAN MOUNDS

ELY FORD MORMON TRAIL CROSSING

SANDY RIDGE

C. BINS

CAMPGROUND

BEACH

Snowmobile Trail
Through Shimek Forest

KEOSAUQUA UNIT - SHIMEK FOREST

2 mi. - HIGHWAY 2

In the 1930s, the Civilian Conservation Corps worked in the park. One of their projects was a shelter built with limestone from an old quarry in the park. A dam was later constructed on Thatcher Creek to form a 30-acre lake in the south central area of the park.

DESCRIPTION: The lake has a boat ramp (electric motors only), a beach for swimming, and a concession stand offering refreshments and boat rental. All are located on the west shore. Hiking trails ring the lake.

The Des Moines River passes through the northern part of the park. Along the river are bluffs of limestone from the Mississippian Period, "St. Louis" Formation, and sandstone probably from the Pennsylvanian Period, Kilbourn Formation. A trail along the river is rich in wildflowers. Indian mounds can be found near the river in the northwestern part of the park.

The park also has meadow areas, valleys, and two natural knobs: Sandy Knob (named after a farmer that went by the name of "Sandy") and Lookout Knob.

Covering 1,600 acres, Lacey-Keosauqua State Park has nearly 20 miles of hiking and nature trails. On the southern edge of the park is the Keosauqua Unit of the Shimek State Forest. In the northwestern area of the park are snowmobile trails, a rental shelter, and picnic areas. The central part of the park has a campground and more picnic areas.

FLORA AND FAUNA: Lacey-Keosauqua is rich in wildlife, including one of the greatest varieties of birds found anywhere in the state. A wide variety of waterfowl can be seen along the river and in the lake area.

The park has an abundance of wildflowers, ferns, trees, shrubs, and other plants. The largest variety of oak trees in the state can be found here, some of which are more than two hundred years old. Pecan trees can also be found.

ACTIVITIES: The park's campground has 160 sites, 45 with electricity, as well as modern restrooms and showers. Also offered in the park are scenic overlooks, cross-country skiing, cabin rental, a boat ramp (electrical motors only), a concession stand, boat rental, hiking, picnicking, nature trails, swimming, and bird-watching. Fishermen can catch crappies and bluegills in the lake and large catfish and flathead catfish in the river. Public hunting is allowed in the state forest area. In the fall, the annual Forest Craft Festival is held here.

ACKNOWLEDGMENT: Wayne Buzzard, park ranger, Lacey-Keosauqua State Park

FOR MORE INFORMATION:

Lacey-Keosauqua State Park. Des Moines: Iowa Department of Natural Resources.

National Park Service, U.S. Department of the Interior. *Mormon Pioneer National Historic Trail*. Washington, D.C.: Government Printing Office, 1981.

Tilden, F. *The State Parks: Their Meaning in American Life*. New York: Alfred A. Knopf, 1962.

Lake Darling State Park

LOCATION: 3 miles west of Brighton on Highways 1 and 78 in Washington County

ADDRESS: R.R. 1, Brighton, Iowa 52540

TELEPHONE: (319) 694-2323

HISTORY: The land for this park was acquired by the state in 1947. Dedication was held on September 17, 1950, and was well attended, including some local bands. On hand to close the valve on the spillway was Jay Norwood "Ding" Darling, for whom the park was named. Darling (1876–1962) was a cartoonist for the *Des Moines Register* and a strong supporter of conservation. His cartoons won him two Pulitzer prizes.

DESCRIPTION: Covering 1,417 acres, Lake Darling State Park has a 302-acre artificial lake fed by Honey Creek. It has a maximum depth of 31 feet. However, only two years after the dedication, a problem with siltation was discovered. The silt accumulated mostly in the northern part of the lake, and eventually the boat dock on that end became useless. The campground, originally located on the north end, was moved to the south end of the lake. A boat dock, hiking trails, and picnic areas are also located in the vicinity.

ACTIVITIES: The 115-site "Cherry Grove" campground is surrounded by a gently sloping landscape. Showers and modern restrooms are present. Thirty-two of the sites have electrical hookups. The campground has become quite popular, and the campers have access to a boat dock. Any size boat motors may be operated at no-wake speeds. For fishermen, there are almost 18 miles of lake shoreline. Channel catfish, carp, largemouth bass, crappies, bluegills, bullheads, and sunfish can be caught.

The park has a supervised beach for swimmers and a bathhouse. A small fee is charged for swimming. There is a concession stand at which refreshments and fishing supplies are available, as well as rental boats and motors. Snowmobiling is permitted in the winter. Playground equipment is present.

The privately owned Lake Darling Youth Center is located on the northeast shore of the lake. With a large lodge and cabins, the center is frequently used by church and school groups.

ACKNOWLEDGMENT: Park ranger, Lake Darling State Park

FOR MORE INFORMATION:

Lake Darling State Park. Des Moines: Iowa Department of Natural Resources.

Lendt, D. L. *Ding, The Life of Jay Norwood Darling.* Ames: Iowa State University Press, 1979.

Lake Keomah State Park

LOCATION: 5 miles east of Oskaloosa on Highway 92, then south and east on Highway 371 for two miles, in Mahaska County

ADDRESS: R.R. 1, Oskaloosa, Iowa 52577

TELEPHONE: (515) 673-6975

HISTORY: Lake Keomah is an artificial lake built in the late 1930s. The maximum depth is 20 feet near the dam located on the northeast end of the lake. Lake Keomah State Park was officially dedicated in 1935. The name "keomah" is a combination of the names Keokuk and Mahaska, the counties that helped finance the park's development.

DESCRIPTION: The park covers 366 acres, including the 84-acre lake. A picnic area, lodge, marina, and beach are located between the two arms of the lake on the south shore. The campground is located near the southern part of the lake. Boat ramps are located on the north and south ends of the lake. Only electric boat motors are permitted. A group camp facility is located at the south end of the park.

The Lake Keomah Fitness Trail encircles the lake and has several exercise stations. There are other hiking trails, also, and the Lake Keomah

71

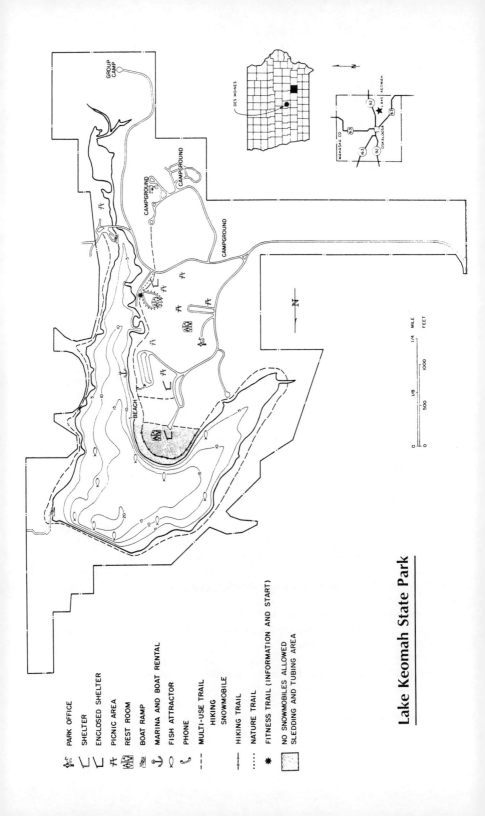

Lake Keomah State Park

Woodland Nature Trail, which is 1/3 of a mile in length.

The park has become very popular, attracting hundreds of thousands of visitors annually.

FLORA: The park is part of the Central Hardwood Forest Region. This region covers most of the eastern one-third of the nation and is rich in oak, hickory, black walnut, black cherry, ash, and cottonwood trees.

ACTIVITIES: The campground has a total of 88 sites, with modern restrooms, showers, and electricity at 52 campsites. A group camp is also present in the park and features a dining hall and group-use building.

For fishermen, the lake offers crappies, bluegills, largemouth bass, and channel catfish. In the winter, snowmobiling is permitted. Other activities include boating, swimming, picnicking, hiking, a fitness trail, and a nature trail. The beautiful lodge, as well as the open shelter, can be reserved for group use.

ACKNOWLEDGMENT: Park ranger, Lake Keomah State Park

FOR MORE INFORMATION:

Lake Keomah Fitness Trail. Des Moines: Iowa Department of Natural Resources.

Lake Keomah State Park. Des Moines: Iowa Department of Natural Resources.

Lake Keomah Woodland Trail. Des Moines: Iowa Department of Natural Resources.

Lake Macbride State Park

LOCATION: 4 miles west of Solon on Highway 382 in Johnson County

ADDRESS: Solon, Iowa 52333

TELEPHONE: (319) 644-2200

HISTORY: In the 1930s, the wooded valleys of Mill Creek and Jordan Creek were recommended for state park status. Pursuing the recommendation were the Iowa City chamber of commerce and J. N. "Ding" Darling, noted Iowa conservationist. In order to raise funds, lots were sold in the

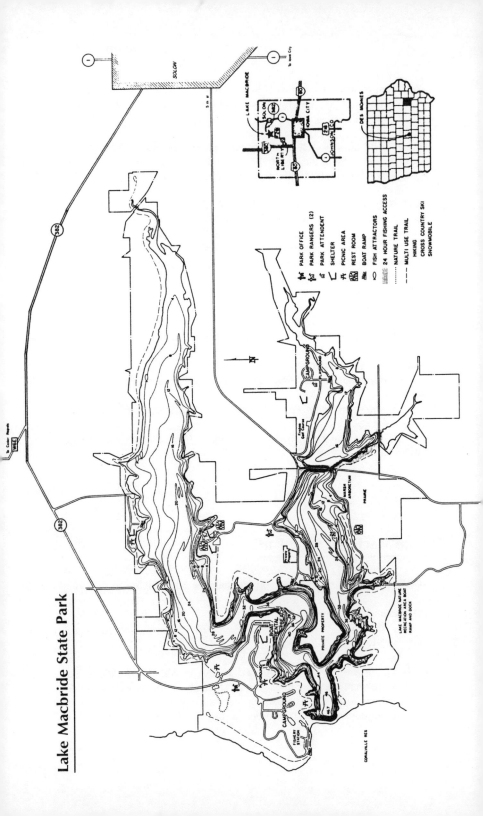

Lake Macbride State Park

area for the construction of private cabins. The funds were then used to purchase additional land in the area for the park.

Although the park was dedicated on May 30, 1934, it was not officially opened to the public until June 15, 1937. Development was accomplished from 1933 to 1938 by the Works Progress Administration and the Civilian Conservation Corps. The name Macbride was selected out of several hundred contest entries. Thomas Huston Macbride was past president of the University of Iowa, a geologist, and a botanist. When the lake was first opened to fishing in 1938, hundreds of anglers caused a massive traffic jam.

When the U.S. Army Corps of Engineers began to plan for the Coralville Reservoir in the 1950s, it was decided that Lake Macbride should remain a separate body of water. To accomplish this, the game fish were removed, and the lake was drained. The old dam was then improved, and a new dam was added. Three years later, in 1960, the new lake was refilled, stocked with fish, and opened for fishing. The park's original facilities had to be moved or rebuilt because of the higher water level. The private cabins were also moved. In 1959 the state acquired more than 1,000 acres from the Corps of Engineers for the park. The "new" Lake Macbride State Park was reopened in May of 1960. The new dam was built under the supervision of the Corps of Engineers.

DESCRIPTION: The rebuilt park has new roads, trails, picnic grounds, restrooms, shelters, expanded campgrounds, and a boat storage area. Jetties were built along the lakeshore for fishing. The lake now covers 812 acres, with a maximum depth of 28 feet. Exposures of the Rapid and Solon members of the Little Cedar Formation (Devonian) occur at the spillway.

The park comprises two units, both of which have been developed for recreation. The north unit is reached via Highway 382 west from Solon. It offers a campground with modern restrooms, showers, and electricity, a beach house with concession stand, supervised swimming, boat rental, boat launching and storage areas, picnic areas, a popular playground, and a state fisheries management station.

The south unit is reached via County Road F-28 west from Solon (Fifth Street in Solon). It offers a marsh, a reestablished prairie, twenty-four–hour fishing accesses, a nonmodern campground (no showers), and Frisbee golf.

FAUNA: Shorebirds and waterfowl are abundant in the park. Long-eared and saw-whet owls can often be seen in the fall and winter.

ACTIVITIES: Lake Macbride has become a popular fishing area with tens of thousands of fishermen annually. Walleye and channel catfish are stocked regularly. Also present are bluegills, largemouth bass, Kentucky spotted bass, crappies, and bullheads.

Today's Lake Macbride State Park draws hundreds of thousands of visitors each year and offers good cross-country skiing, snowmobiling, boating of many types, bird-watching, hiking, Frisbee golf, picnicking, fishing, and swimming. Mushroom hunting is popular. There is a ten horsepower limit on boat motors from May 21 to September 7. At other times, any size motors may be operated at no-wake speeds. The supervised beach and the concession stand are especially popular.

With a total of 122 campsites (40 with electricity), the park offers both nonmodern and modern camping. The modern campground has electricity, modern restrooms, and showers. Information on fishing here can be obtained from the Fisheries Biologist, Macbride Fisheries Station, Box 236, Solon, Iowa 52333.

The 5-mile-long Solon–Lake Macbride multiuse trail runs from the north shore of the lake, east to the nearby town of Solon, and is popular with bicyclists and walkers.

ACKNOWLEDGMENT: Staff, Lake Macbride State Park

FOR MORE INFORMATION:
Lake Macbride State Park. Des Moines: Iowa Department of Natural Resources.

Plocher, O. W., and B. J. Bunker. *Geologic Reconnaissance of the Coralville Lake Area.* Iowa City: Geological Society of Iowa, 1989.

Lake Wapello State Park

LOCATION: 6 miles west of Drakesville on Highway 273 in Davis County

ADDRESS: Drakesville, Iowa 52552

TELEPHONE: (515) 722-3371

HISTORY: Lake Wapello State Park was acquired by the state in the early 1930s and was officially named in April of 1933. The Civilian Conservation Corps developed the park in the 1930s. One of its projects was the construction of a dam with a berm that traps sediment and allows the clear water to flow into the lake.

DESCRIPTION: The park covers 1,168 acres, including the 284-acre lake. Much of the surrounding land is ruggedly timbered.

Lake Wapello State Park

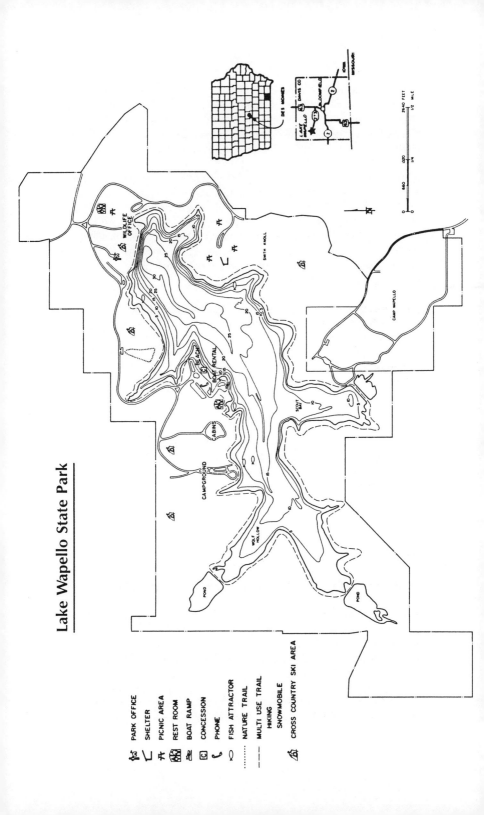

PARK OFFICE
SHELTER
PICNIC AREA
REST ROOM
BOAT RAMP
CONCESSION
PHONE
FISH ATTRACTOR
NATURE TRAIL
MULTI USE TRAIL
    HIKING
    SNOWMOBILE
CROSS COUNTRY SKI AREA

FLORA AND FAUNA: The park has dense areas of woods, primarily white oak and bur oak, but several other trees and shrubs are also present. Wildlife abounds at Lake Wapello. Everything from songbirds and small mammals to white-tailed deer and wild turkeys can be found here. There is a thriving beaver population, as witnessed by the number of downed trees.

ACTIVITIES: The park offers boating (any size boat motors may be operated at no-wake speeds), supervised swimming, a concession stand, cross-country skiing, fishing (bass, crappies, bluegills, channel catfish), picnicking, playground equipment, hiking, snowmobiling, a nature trail (Lake Wapello Interpretive Trail), and thirteen rental cabins. At the concession stand, the public can rent paddleboats, canoes, fishing boats, and boat motors. The park also has an 88-site campground with modern restrooms and showers, and 44 sites with electricity.

ACKNOWLEDGMENT: Park ranger, Lake Wapello State Park

FOR MORE INFORMATION:
Lake Wapello Interpretive Trail. Des Moines: Iowa Department of Natural Resources.

Oakland Mills State Park

LOCATION: 4 miles southwest of Mount Pleasant on County Road W-55 in Henry County

ADDRESS: Henry County Conservation Board, Mount Pleasant, Iowa 52641

TELEPHONE: (319) 986-5067 (Henry County Conservation Board)

HISTORY: In 1839 Robert and James Wilson built a dam and a flour mill on the Skunk River at the site of a small fishing village known as Oakland Mills. The mill became known as Wilson Mill and was four stories high. A permit was granted by the state of Wisconsin to build the mill. At that time, Wisconsin had jurisdiction over the area. The mill was demolished in 1910, and the Iowa Electric Light and Power Company purchased the dam. In 1924 the company built a new dam 300 feet farther downstream.

The park was made possible by a series of purchases and gifts in 1919 and 1920. Several local people sold land to the state at a cost of between 180 to 200 dollars per acre. Additional land was donated by another land-owner, the Oakland Cemetery Association, and the Oakland Club. The town of Oakland Mills was adjacent to the park.

DESCRIPTION: Eighty-four acres of the park are owned by the state and have been managed by the Henry County Conservation Board since 1970. An additional 24 acres are owned by the county. A large bluff is present along the road near the Skunk River and exposes Mississippian-Period lime-stone, shale, and sandstone of the Keokuk, Warsaw, Spergen, and "St. Louis" formations.

The headquarters of the Henry County Conservation Board is located in the park.

ACTIVITIES: The park has wooded hills, hiking trails, bridle trails, and pic-nic areas. Fishing and boating can be done in the Skunk River. There is also a campground, but it lacks electrical hookups.

ACKNOWLEDGMENT: Don Peak, Henry County Conservation Board, Oakland Mills State Park

Odessa Campground

LOCATION: 6 miles north of Toolesboro on County Road X-61 in Louisa County

ADDRESS: Louisa County Conservation Board, Wapello, Iowa 52653

TELEPHONE: (319) 523-8381 (Louisa County Conservation Board)

HISTORY: Before the first settlers arrived, the present-day Odessa Wildlife Area was visited by Ioway, Illinois, and Sac and Fox Indians. When the Marquette and Joliet expedition arrived here on June 25, 1673, they found two Indian villages in the vicinity of present-day Toolesboro (originally known as Blackhawk). Indian mounds here have been declared a national historic monument, known as the Toolesboro Indian Mounds.

The first settlers arrived in 1835. In the years that followed, numerous towns appeared in the area. One of these was Burris City, which was founded in 1855. Farming in the area was already extensive. Wheat, oats, rye, corn, potatoes, mustard seed, pork, meat, and lard were being exported via the Mississippi River. However, the town declined rapidly and was abandoned in 1858. Nothing remains of the town today, which was located in the southernmost part of the Odessa Wildlife Area.

The state acquired the first part of the land in 1946. The area was taken out of farming and allowed to return to its natural state. Waterfowl and other wildlife returned, and Odessa became popular with waterfowl hunters and other outdoorsmen.

DESCRIPTION: The 4-acre campground is located at Snively Access, a wildlife management area within the Odessa Wildlife Area. The wildlife area (6,000 acres) extends almost 8 miles along the Mississippi River and has bluffs, lakes, ponds, creeks, marshes, and forested islands. Lock and Dam 17, built in 1939, is located in the vicinity. South of the DNR wildlife management area headquarters, along the west shore of Lake Odessa, is the Snively Access with the Odessa Campground.

FAUNA: The area is visited by hundreds of thousands of migrating birds, including mallards, wood ducks, and the greatest concentrations of Canadian geese in the state. Other birds include bald eagles, osprey, and pileated woodpeckers. Deer are also common.

ACTIVITIES: The campground has 36 sites, a dozen of which have electrical hookups. There are also picnic areas, and a boat ramp and boat rental are located in the vicinity. There is no restriction on horsepower for boat motors. Fishing is offered in Lake Odessa, especially for bluegills and crappies. Canoeing is popular in the Mississippi River backwaters and in Burris Ditch.

Waterfowl, deer, and squirrel hunting are permitted in the wildlife area. For more information on hunting, contact the DNR, Lake Odessa Unit, R.R. 1, Wapello, Iowa 52653.

ACKNOWLEDGMENTS: Jim Rudisill, executive director, Louisa County Conservation Board, Wapello, Iowa

Bill Ohde, district management biologist, Wapello, Iowa

FOR MORE INFORMATION:

Odessa Wildlife Area Controlled Waterfowl Hunting. Des Moines: Iowa Department of Natural Resources.

Plum Grove

LOCATION: Take Lower Muscatine Road north and west from Highway 6 in southeast Iowa City. Turn west on Kirkwood Avenue and continue to Carroll Street. Turn south to the site (Johnson County).

ADDRESS: 1030 Carroll Street, Iowa City, Iowa 52240

TELEPHONE: (319) 895-6039

HISTORY: In 1838 Robert Lucas, a Quaker and Democrat, was appointed Iowa's first governor by President Martin Van Buren. He served only one term, however, being removed from office by the Harrison-Tyler administration in 1841. He was a veteran of the War of 1812 and served as a state representative and state senator in Ohio.

Lucas built Plum Grove in 1844, using stone from a local quarry and brick manufactured in Iowa City. The home had seven main rooms, each with a fireplace, and was built on 80 acres of land. He died in the home on February 7, 1853, and was buried in Oakland Cemetery in Iowa City. The Lucases had three children—Mary, Edward, and Robert, Jr.

The home and 4 acres of land were purchased by the state in 1940 and dedicated as a historical shrine on November 2, 1946. It has been restored and was furnished by the National Society of Colonial Dames in Iowa, using 1840s furniture.

DESCRIPTION: Plum Grove is a 4-acre piece of land with a redbrick building built by Robert Lucas, Iowa's first governor. He designed the home, surrounded by plum trees, after his old home in Ohio.

The home is open from mid-April through mid-October, 1:00 P.M. to 5:00 P.M., Wednesday through Sunday.

ACKNOWLEDGMENT: Staff at Plum Grove

FOR MORE INFORMATION:
Plum Grove. Des Moines: Iowa Department of Natural Resources.

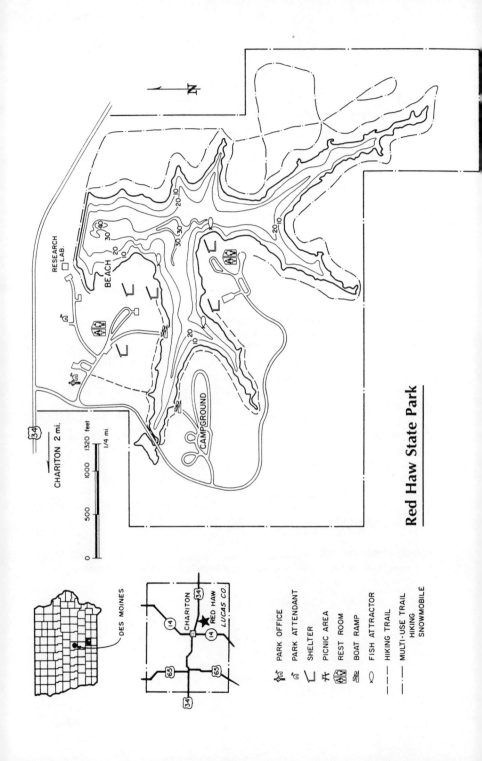

Red Haw State Park

Red Haw State Park

LOCATION: 2 miles east of Chariton off Highway 34 in Lucas County

ADDRESS: Chariton, Iowa 50049

TELEPHONE: (515) 774-5632

HISTORY: The first white settlers here were Mormons in 1846. However, they soon moved westward. In 1847 the William McDermott family became the first permanent settlers. Their homestead was located about 8 miles east of the present park.

In 1934 the state began work on a lake and a park here. The cost of the original park development was five thousand dollars. The main purpose of the lake was to serve as a backup source of water for the town of Chariton.

DESCRIPTION: Today the park covers 420 acres, including the 64-acre lake. The lake reaches its greatest depth of 40 feet at the dam on the north shore.

In 1971 a supervised beach facility costing eighty-three thousand dollars and a parking lot were completed just northwest of the dam. At the beach is a concession stand where refreshments are available and boats can be rented. A picnic area with an open shelter is also located here. From the shelter, visitors have a scenic view of the lake and of Lake Ellis to the north.

An 86-unit campground is located west of the lake and has electrical hookups (at 60 sites), modern restrooms, and showers. A boat ramp and trailer parking area are nearby. In the south central area of the lake is another picnic area with an open shelter. A Department of Natural Resources fisheries research station is present at the north end of the park near the dam.

FLORA AND FAUNA: Red Haw Lake is named after the abundance of red haw trees in the area. Early May is one of the best times to visit the park, when the red haws and redbuds are in bloom. There is also abundant wildlife.

ACTIVITIES: Bluegills, largemouth bass, channel catfish, and crappies can be caught in the lake. Grass carp have been introduced to cut down on vegetation growth.

The park also offers boating (electric motors only), boat rental, scenic views, supervised swimming, a concession stand, two rental shelters, a popular playground, camping, hiking, and snowmobiling.

ACKNOWLEDGMENT: Staff at the State Archives

83

Rock Creek State Park

LOCATION: 3 miles north of Kellogg on Highway 224, then 3 miles east on County Road F-27, in Jasper County

ADDRESS: R.R. 2, Box 99, Kellogg, Iowa 50135

TELEPHONE: (515) 236-3722

HISTORY: Rock Creek State Park was developed in the 1950s to provide citizens in the vicinity with a recreation area. Until Red Rock Lake was constructed in the 1960s, Rock Creek Lake was the only major body of water in this area. The park was officially dedicated on August 24, 1952.

DESCRIPTION: Excluding the Corps of Engineers reservoirs, Rock Creek Lake is the sixth largest artificial lake in the state. It covers 602 acres with 15 miles of shoreline. Near the dam in the southern part, the lake reaches its greatest depth of 32 feet. The dam—1,650 feet long and 34 feet high—provides a scenic view of the lake, which is fed by Rock Creek.

The park covers 1,267 acres and has a 232-site campground along the east shore of the lake. Forty-six of the sites have electrical hookups. Some of the campsites are situated on the shore, and others overlook the lake. Modern restrooms and showers are present.

The Rock Creek Wildlife Management Area is next to the park. It is comprised mostly of upland habitat with portions of timber and marsh—shallow lake habitats. Public hunting is allowed there.

The park is located only 6 miles north and 3 miles east of Interstate 80, exit 45.

FAUNA: There is abundant wildlife, including deer, pheasants, rabbits, and thousands of migrating ducks, mainly teal, and mallards.

ACTIVITIES: Hiking, snowmobiling, and bridle trails surround the lake, except in the northernmost end. A nature trail is present, and there are a total of five boat ramps around the lake (any size boat motors are permitted at no-wake speeds). Other activities include camping, scenic views, picnicking, playground equipment, swimming, and bird-watching. Waterfowl, pheasant, and rabbit hunting are permitted nearby in the Rock Creek Wildlife Management Area.

For fishermen, bluegills, largemouth bass, crappies, channel catfish, walleyes, white bass, tiger muskies, northern pike, and bullheads are present.

ACKNOWLEDGMENT: Larry Aldridge, park ranger, Rock Creek State Park

FOR MORE INFORMATION:
Rock Creek State Park. Des Moines: Iowa Department of Natural Resources.

Sharon Bluffs State Park

LOCATION: 3½ miles east and south of Centerville off Highway 2 in Appanoose County

ADDRESS: Appanoose County Conservation Board, Centerville, Iowa 52544

TELEPHONE: (515) 856-8528 (Appanoose County Conservation Board)

HISTORY: Originally called "Chariton Bluffs," the first 25 acres of this park were purchased from W. M. Evans by the Association of Commerce of Centerville on November 25, 1929, at a cost of $1,375. In 1930 the same organization proposed that the state purchase an additional 121 acres from Mr. Evans at a cost of $6,000. The name "Sharon" comes from a pioneer town by that name in the vicinity. The town was believed to have been named by Mormons. As the nearby towns of Centerville and Chaldea grew, Sharon declined and eventually was abandoned.

ACTIVITIES: The present-day 144-acre Sharon Bluffs State Park offers camping, hiking, picnicking, and fishing in the Chariton River.

ACKNOWLEDGMENT: Staff, Iowa Department of Natural Resources

Shimek State Forest

LOCATION: 1 mile east of Farmington on Highway 2 in Lee County

ADDRESS: Farmington, Iowa 52626

TELEPHONE: (319) 878-3811

HISTORY: The Shimek State Forest was named in 1950 after Bohumil Shimek (1861–1937). Shimek was a professor of botany, head of the University of Iowa's Botany Department, and director of the Iowa Lakeside Laboratory. The first 4,000 acres were purchased in the mid-1930s. During World War II, several smaller purchases were made. In 1964 an additional 3,000 acres were purchased from the U.S. Forest Service by the state. Since then, there have been other smaller purchases.

DESCRIPTION: Today this is the largest forest owned by the state of Iowa. It covers 8,762 acres and consists of five units:

- Croton Unit covers 1,707 acres and is located 2 miles south and 1 mile east of Croton.
- Lick Creek Unit covers 2,841 acres to the south of the Donnellson Unit and northeast of Croton.
- Farmington Unit covers 2,098 acres north and east of Farmington.
- Donnellson Unit covers 1,223 acres to the east of the Farmington Unit, about 6 miles west of Donnellson on Highway 2.
- Keosauqua Unit covers 893 acres adjacent to the Lacey-Keosauqua State Park, 3 miles southwest of Keosauqua in Van Buren County.

Extensive pine tree planting has been carried out in the forest, beginning in 1939 with the Civilian Conservation Corps. About a dozen varieties are present.

FLORA AND FAUNA: The forest has a large variety of pine trees, abundant wildlife, including many songbirds, and a large number of wildflowers.

ACTIVITIES: The Farmington, Donnellson, and Lick Creek units have been developed for public use. There is a total of seven artificial ponds for fishing, and they have been stocked with largemouth bass, crappies, bluegills, and other panfish. Activities offered include camping, picnicking, bridle trails, hiking trails, a nature trail, cross-country skiing, snowmobiling, boat ramps (electric boat motors only), scenic views, and hunting for squirrels, quail, deer, rabbits, and turkeys. The turkeys were introduced in 1965.

They have spread from the original eleven released in the Lick Creek Unit into the other units and surrounding land.

There is a total of 50 campsites in the forest, but they lack electricity, modern restrooms, and showers. Water is available at the forest headquarters, which is located 1 mile northeast of Farmington in the northern part of the Farmington Unit.

Additional picnic and camping areas and more ponds are planned for the Farmington and Donnellson units. The Croton, Lick Creek, and Keosauqua units will be left for timber production and wildlife habitat.

ACKNOWLEDGMENT: Wayne H. Fuhlbrugge, area forester, Shimek State Forest

FOR MORE INFORMATION:
Shimek State Forest. Des Moines: Iowa Department of Natural Resources.

Starrs Cave Park and Preserve

LOCATION: Northern edge of Burlington along Irish Ridge Road in Des Moines County

ADDRESS: Starrs Cave Nature Center, Burlington, Iowa 52601

TELEPHONE: (319) 753-5808 (Starrs Cave Nature Center)

HISTORY: Before the first settlers arrived, this land was considered to be "neutral ground" among the Indians. They collected flint here for use in making arrowheads and tools. In the early 1800s, a trading post was established here by Colonel Johnson of the American Fur Company. Early pioneers traded furs with Indians at the post until around 1812. Remains of the old post are still present.

The first landowners were members of the Manson family from Burlington. They arrived in the 1840s. The first known discovery of caves here by settlers was in May 1858. Stolen items were found in the largest cave, and it was believed that a gang had been hiding out there. In later years, rumors state that the Jesse James gang used the area. Before the Civil War, the site was a station in the Underground Railroad.

William Starr obtained ownership of the land in the 1860s. His original

87

house still stands in the park, as do the rock walls of an old barn.

Around the turn of the century, the Dunn family acquired the land. An attempt to turn the area into a state park as early as 1924 failed because of opposition from local residents. Not until August 1974 did the state finally acquire the land. The 142-acre tract was purchased at that time from Herb and Alice Dunn. In 1975 the Des Moines County Conservation Board agreed to manage the park. Although bought with state funds, the tract was never a state park but was immediately transferred under long-term lease to the county conservation board. An old barn built in the 1920s was converted into a nature center in 1982. As late as the early 1970s, the barn had served as an inn, the Sycamore Inn.

DESCRIPTION: The park covers 142 acres and has a nature center and an old house. The house was built by William Starr in the 1860s. Both buildings are located in the eastern part.

There are numerous caves and tunnels in the park's bluffs, some of which have not been rediscovered. The bluffs rise above the north bank of Flint Creek. They are accessible via a hiking trail off Irish Ridge Road about ½ mile north of the bridge over the creek. The largest cave, Starrs Cave, extends for at least 100 feet and is used occasionally by little brown bats. A limestone overhang is known as Devil's Kitchen. A scenic view is offered, 200 feet above the creek.

The bluffs expose shale, limestone, and dolomitic limestone of several Mississippian-Period formations: McCraney, Prospect Hill, Starrs Cave, Wassonville, and Burlington. Along the creek is exposed siltstone of the Devonian period, English River formation. The park has one of the best exposures of Starrs Cave limestone in the state.

FLORA AND FAUNA: Starrs Cave Park and Preserve is home to a large variety of wildlife, especially deer and wood ducks. Little brown bats sometimes inhabit the larger caves.

The park has a floodplain forest, a maple-basswood forest, and an oak-hickory forest. There are also small prairie areas and meadows in the park that have prairie grasses. Wildflowers can be found in abundance.

ACTIVITIES: The Starrs Cave Nature Center is open on Sundays from 2:00 to 5:00 P.M. and at other times by appointment. Observation areas, restrooms, and a small library are included. The staff provides a wide variety of specially tailored educational programs and activities for youth groups and classes.

The park is open all year from 6:00 A.M. until 10:30 P.M. Activities offered include scenic views, cave exploring, hiking, photography, bird-watching, cross-country skiing, and nature study. Picnicking is permitted only in the vicinity of the nature center. Because the area is also a preserve, there are several activities that are prohibited, such as camping, horseback riding, any kind of off-road vehicle traffic, hunting, trapping, fishing, mushroom hunting, bluff climbing, and straying off the trails. Collecting anything within the park is strictly prohibited.

ACKNOWLEDGMENT: Staff at the Starrs Cave Nature Center

FOR MORE INFORMATION:
Starrs Cave Park and Preserve. Burlington: Des Moines County Conservation Board.

Stephens State Forest

LOCATION: Lucas Unit campground is 1 mile west of Lucas and just south of Highway 34 in Lucas County; White Breast Unit campground is 2 miles south of Lucas on Highway 65 and 2 miles west on a county road in Lucas County.

ADDRESS: R.R. 3, Box 31, Chariton, Iowa 50049

TELEPHONE: (515) 774-5632

DESCRIPTION: Stephens State Forest was established in the 1930s and named after Dr. T. C. Stephens, who was a highly respected teacher from Sioux City. The forest consists of six separate units, totalling 9,202 acres. These units are:

- Cedar Creek Unit covers 1,007 acres and is located 4 miles east and 1 mile south of Williamson in Lucas County.
- Chariton Unit covers 1,185 acres and is located 6 miles east of Williamson in Lucas County.
- Lucas Unit covers 991 acres and is located 1 mile west of Lucas just south of Highway 34 in Lucas County.
- Thousand Acre Unit covers 884 acres and is located 7 miles east and 1 mile north of Williamson in Lucas and Monroe counties.
- Unionville Unit covers 1,879 acres spread out over eight small areas to the north and east of Unionville in Appanoose and Davis counties.
- White Breast Unit covers 3,256 acres in two areas, 2 miles south and 2 miles west of Lucas in Lucas County, and 2½ miles south of Woodburn in Clarke County.

Of all the units, Lucas and White Breast have been developed the most for recreational use. Campgrounds are located in both units. Both units also have two large ponds that have been stocked with largemouth bass, bluegills, and channel catfish. Only electric boat motors are permitted on the ponds. Smaller fishing ponds can be found in the White Breast, Cedar Creek, and Chariton units.

The western part of the White Breast Unit has hiking and cross-country skiing trails. Snowmobiling trails can be found throughout the White Breast and Lucas units. A backpack trail was established in the southwestern part of the White Breast Unit. The trail requires two to three hours to complete one way, and campsites are available.

Exposed along streams in the forest is glacial till of the Nebraskan and Kansan glacial stages and loess of the Wisconsin Glacial Stage.

FLORA AND FAUNA: Both upland and bottomland (floodplain) forests are represented. Prairie grasses can be found in the open areas of the forest. There is an abundance of wildlife, including a wide variety of birds, especially songbirds and predatory birds.

ACTIVITIES: There is a total of 60 campsites without modern facilities or electricity. No fee is charged in the backpack camping area. Other activities include fishing, picnicking, hunting (deer, squirrel, rabbit, raccoon, quail, and turkey—introduced in 1968), snowmobiling, nature study, mushroom hunting, bridle trails, and bird-watching. Hunting is prohibited in the camping areas. Horses are prohibited in the picnic areas.

ACKNOWLEDGMENT: Duane A. Bedford, district forester, Chariton

FOR MORE INFORMATION:
   Stephens State Forest. Des Moines: Iowa Department of Natural Resources.
   Stephens State Forest Backpacking Trails. Des Moines: Iowa Department of Natural Resources.

Wildcat Den State Park

LOCATION: 3 miles east of Fairport off Highway 22 in Muscatine County

ADDRESS: R.R. 3, Box 170, Muscatine, Iowa 52761

TELEPHONE: (319) 263-4337

HISTORY: Wildcat Den is a cave in the center of the present park, which, as legend has it, was at one time occupied by bobcats. An attack on a young boy by one of the cats was recorded in 1856. The boy managed to escape. There probably are no bobcats remaining in the park, but several of the caves that they once used can be seen.

In 1905 Emma and Clara Brandt purchased the property. They set the land aside as a preserve and provided a watchman. In 1927 they donated 67 acres to the state to develop a state park. The state acquired an additional 141 acres, including the Pine Creek gristmill. The mill was built by Benjamin Nye in 1848 and was included in the National Register of Historic Places in 1980. Nye was buried in a cemetery near the mill. A bronze plaque was placed in the center of the park in memory of the Brandts.

DESCRIPTION: Today Wildcat Den State Park covers 417 acres. In the central area of the park, above the old mill, is a 32-site, nonmodern campground. A shelter, which may be reserved, was built in the 1930s by the CCC. Oak, pine, and walnut trees shade this area of the park.

Hiking trails can be found throughout the central areas, and one trail provides access to the eastern part where the mill and a restored, turn-of-the-century country schoolhouse are located. Some sights are accessible only by hiking, but visitors are advised not to stray off the marked trails. Drop-offs of up to 100 feet can be concealed by dense brush.

The Wildcat Den Interpretive Trail is 1½ miles in length and requires one hour of walking. At times, the trail can be tiring. In addition to the Brandt memorial and Wildcat Den, the trail also takes hikers past a scenic view that overlooks the surrounding countryside; "Devil's Punch Bowl," which has iron-stained water flowing from a spring; "Horseshoe Bend," a curve in Pine Creek; "Fat Man's Squeeze," once a narrow passage through rock that has been widened by shifting rocks; and "Steamboat Rock," which is a bluff that resembles a steamboat.

The park has one of the best exposures of the Wildcat Den Coal Member of the Caseyville Formation, Pennsylvanian Period. This exposure consists of coal and shale overlaid with sandstone. The sandstone has been referred to as the "Spoon Formation" and is also Pennsylvanian in age. However, recent studies indicate that this rock may be the southeastern

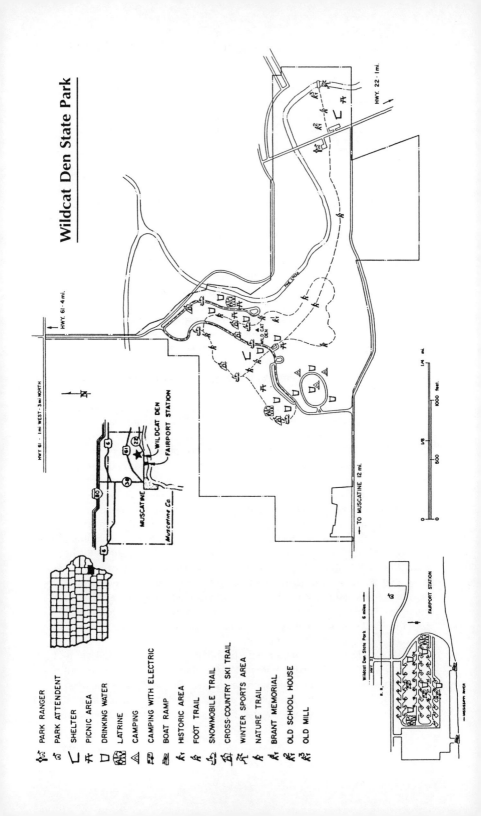

Wildcat Den State Park

HWY. 61 - 4 mi.

HWY. 61 - 1 mi WEST - 3 mi NORTH

HWY. 22 - 1 mi.

WILD CAT DEN

WILDCAT DEN FAIRPORT STATION

MUSCATINE

Muscatine Co.

← TO MUSCATINE 12 mi.

0   500   1000 feet   1/8   1/4 mi.

Wildcat Den State Park — 6 miles — HWY. 22

FAIRPORT STATION

MISSISSIPPI RIVER

- 🛈 PARK RANGER
- 🛈 PARK ATTENDENT
- ⌐ SHELTER
- ⅄ PICNIC AREA
- ⬜ DRINKING WATER
- 🏠 LATRINE
- △ CAMPING
- ⛺ CAMPING WITH ELECTRIC
- ⛵ BOAT RAMP
- 🛈 HISTORIC AREA
- 🛈 FOOT TRAIL
- 🛈 SNOWMOBILE TRAIL
- 🛈 CROSS COUNTRY SKI TRAIL
- 🛈 WINTER SPORTS AREA
- 🛈 NATURE TRAIL
- 🛈 BRANT MEMORIAL
- 🛈 OLD SCHOOL HOUSE
- 🛈 OLD MILL

Iowa equivalent to the Floris Formation, which is exposed in central and southern Iowa.

Six miles to the west of Wildcat Den State Park, on Highway 22 along the Mississippi River, is the Fairport Station Recreation Area, which features a modern campground and boat ramps.

FLORA AND FAUNA: The park is dominated by upland forest, primarily oaks and hickories. Some of the pines and oaks are between 100 and 150 years old. On the floor of the forest and along the bluffs can be found at least twenty-five varieties of ferns. Wildflowers and wildlife can be found in abundance. Bald eagles are seen occasionally.

ACTIVITIES: The park offers camping, stream fishing, hiking, public viewing of the historic 1848 mill and country schoolhouse, scenic views, picnicking, snowmobiling, cross-country skiing, and an interpretive trail.

ACKNOWLEDGMENT: Beverly Reasoner, park attendant, Wildcat Den State Park

FOR MORE INFORMATION:

Wildcat Den Interpretive Trail. Des Moines: Iowa Department of Natural Resources.

Wildcat Den State Park. Des Moines: Iowa Department of Natural Resources.

3 Southwest Iowa

Pammel State Park entrance tunnel dug in the late 1850s and later expanded.

Camping facilities at Springbrook State Park.

Fishing from the ford at Pammel State Park.

State park picnic opportunities abound. (Pammel)

About two hundred deer roam Springbrook State Park and are easily seen.

Badger Creek State Recreation Area

LOCATION: 5 miles south of West Des Moines on Interstate 35, then 5 miles west on County Road G-14, in Madison County

ADDRESS: Walnut Woods State Park, Box 133, R.R. 3, Des Moines, Iowa 50321

TELEPHONE: (515) 285-4502 (Walnut Woods State Park)

DESCRIPTION: Badger Creek is a recently acquired area of 1,162 acres, including a 276-acre artificial lake. The habitat is a combination of lake and upland. There is very little forest on the area. A modern boat ramp and parking area are located on each side of the lake for boater convenience. On the east side are picnic areas with two open shelters and nonmodern restroom facilities. The west end of the lake remains undeveloped, to provide wildlife habitat and public hunting opportunities. A small pond is located on the north edge of the area and provides panfish fishing.

ACTIVITIES: The area offers fishing, boating (any size boat motors may be used at no-wake speeds), hiking, picnicking, and hunting for pheasant, rabbit, waterfowl, deer, and quail.

ACKNOWLEDGMENT: Scot Michelson, park ranger, Walnut Woods State Park

Barkley State Forest

LOCATION: 2 miles northeast of Fraser on a county road in Boone County

HISTORY: The Barkley State Forest was donated to the state in 1929 by E. and Spencer Barkley. For many years, the forest was under the management of the State Parks Section, until recently, when it was transferred to the State Forestry Section, which can more efficiently manage the site.

DESCRIPTION: The 40-acre forest is located along breaks in the Des Moines River about 5 miles north of Boone. It is very similar in geology, flora, and fauna to the Holst State Forest.

99

ACTIVITIES: Activities are quite limited here, but hunting and nature study are permitted. However, the forest is surrounded by privately owned land, and permission must be obtained from adjacent landowners to get to this site.

ACKNOWLEDGMENT: James Bulman, regional forester, Ames, Iowa

Big Creek State Park

LOCATION: 2 miles north of Polk City on County Road R-38 in Polk County

ADDRESS: R.R. 1, Polk City, Iowa 50226

TELEPHONE: (515) 984-6473

HISTORY: In 1972 Big Creek Lake (905 acres) was created. It was a cooperative project by the Iowa Conservation Commission and the U.S. Army Corps of Engineers, which leased 1,536 acres to the state. This land became Big Creek State Park.

DESCRIPTION: A bicycle trail along the east side of the lake provides good cross-country skiing and snowmobiling during the winter. The trail travels south of the park through the Saylorville Lake area and all the way to the Birdland Park Marina in Des Moines. It has become one of the most popular bicycle trails in Iowa.

To the west and north of the park is a wildlife management area providing upland habitat for wildlife. Pheasant, quail, deer, rabbit, and squirrel can be hunted here. The lake itself is popular for waterfowl hunting.

In the 1970s, largemouth bass, muskellunge, channel catfish, blue catfish, walleyes, bluegills, and crappies were stocked. Smallmouth bass were already present in the old creek channel. Tiger muskie have also been stocked. Ice fishing is very popular here.

There are several boat ramps located outside the park. These are open for public use twenty-four hours a day.

ACTIVITIES: The park offers picnicking (with many shelters that may be reserved), swimming, a concession stand, bicycling, playgrounds, sports fields, hiking, cross-country skiing, snowmobiling, boat and boat motor rental, and fishing. A large handicapped-accessible fishing pier was added

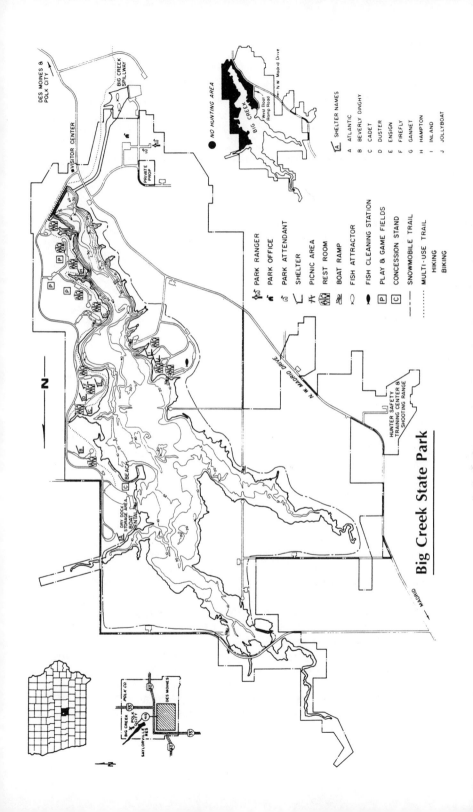

Big Creek State Park

SHELTER NAMES

- A ATLANTIC
- B BEVERLY DINGHY
- C CADET
- D DUSTER
- E ENSIGN
- F FIREFLY
- G GANNET
- H HAMPTON
- I INLAND
- J JOLLYBOAT

NO HUNTING AREA

PARK RANGER
PARK OFFICE
PARK ATTENDANT
SHELTER
PICNIC AREA
REST ROOM
BOAT RAMP
FISH ATTRACTOR
FISH CLEANING STATION
PLAY & GAME FIELDS
CONCESSION STAND
SNOWMOBILE TRAIL
MULTI-USE TRAIL
HIKING
BIKING

DES MOINES &
POLK CITY

BIG CREEK SPILLWAY

VISITOR CENTER

PRIVATE PROP

N.W. Madrid Drive
West Boat Ramp Road
BIG CREEK

N.W. MADRID DRIVE

MADRID

HUNTER SAFETY
TRAINING CENTER &
SHOOTING RANGE

BEACH

DRY DOCK
STORAGE AREA
BOAT RENTAL

POLK CO.
BIG CREEK
POLK CITY
DES MOINES
SAYLORVILLE PARK

in 1990. The park has four modern boat ramps. From May 21 to September 7, the maximum motor size is ten horsepower. At other times, any size motors may be used at no-wake speeds. Hunting is permitted outside the park in the wildlife management area.

ACKNOWLEDGMENT: Rod Slings, park ranger, Big Creek State Park

Cold Springs State Park

LOCATION: 1 mile south of Lewis on County Road M-56 in Cass County

ADDRESS: Cass County Conservation Board, Atlantic, Iowa 50022

TELEPHONE: (712) 243-3542 (Cass County Conservation Board)

HISTORY: Before the first settlers arrived, this area was a popular gathering ground for Indians. The first settlers were Jehu and Jane Woodward in 1856. At that time, a deep creek flowed into the Nishnabotna River here. The land was situated on the Mormon Trail and was used as a campground by the travelers.

In 1896–97, Jehu built a lake (Crystal Lake) in the area, and it quickly became a popular recreation area. During the Depression, local citizens raised five thousand dollars to purchase the land and turn it over to the state to develop a park. In 1938 the state acquired the land, but development of the park came to a halt and existing facilities were neglected. This was in part due to the Depression and World War II. The buildings were demolished and the lake dried up.

Not until 1948 did a new effort begin to develop a state park. Work on a new artificial lake and park facilities was started in 1949. The work took slightly more than a year, and in June 1951, Cold Springs State Park became a reality. The park has been managed by the Cass County Conservation Board since the early 1960s.

DESCRIPTION: The 16-acre lake and most of the park's facilities are located in the southeastern half of the 104-acre park. The northwestern half contains a marsh, an old floodplain forest, and a dried-up oxbow lake, once the channel of the Nishnabotna River. A large forested area to the north of the lake is on the floodplain of the river. The new river channel runs along the western boundary of the park. In this area, the river cuts through limestone and shale of the Pennsylvanian Period, Oread Formation: Leavenworth, Heebner, Plattsmouth, Heumader, and Kereford members. The Plattsmouth limestone, Heumader shale, and Kereford limestone are quite fossiliferous here, and the exposures occur outside the park boundary.

The park serves as the southwest headquarters for the Fish and Wildlife Division of the Department of Natural Resources.

ACTIVITIES: Today Cold Springs State Park has a campground with electricity, a picnic area with horseshoe courts and an enclosed shelter, playground equipment, trails for hiking and snowmobiling, an artificial lake that offers boating (electric motors only) and fishing, and a beach for swimmers.

ACKNOWLEDGMENT: Melanie Hayner, naturalist, Cass County Conservation Board, Atlantic

FOR MORE INFORMATION:
National Park Service, U.S. Department of the Interior. *Mormon Pioneer National Historic Trail.* Washington, D.C.: Government Printing Office, 1981.

Gifford State Forest

LOCATION: Southern edge of Council Bluffs in Pottawattamie County, 2 miles west of Lake Manawa, just south of Highway 92

HISTORY: This forest was donated to the state in 1942 by the Gifford family in memory of Dr. Harold Gifford. The family wanted to preserve what had become a nesting site for great blue herons. However, due to increased activity at neighboring airports, and to the growing population of Council Bluffs, the herons started to abandon the area, and by the mid-1950s, they were gone for good. In 1970 the land was transferred to the Forestry Section from the Wildlife Section, both part of the Iowa Conservation Commission.

DESCRIPTION: Lying within the city limits of Council Bluffs, the 40-acre forest is preserved primarily for observation and management studies. It is not developed for recreational use.

FLORA: Located on the Missouri River floodplain, this is a floodplain forest with a great abundance of cottonwood trees and several other types of trees.

ACKNOWLEDGMENT: Allan L. Pratt, district forester, Red Oak

Green Valley State Park

LOCATION: 3 miles north of Creston on Highway 186 in Union County

ADDRESS: Creston, Iowa 50801

TELEPHONE: (515) 782-5131

HISTORY: One of the communities hard hit by the drought of the 1930s was Creston. Its reservoir, Summit Lake, dried up completely in 1934. Steps taken to prevent further problems included the construction of a new 390-acre lake, designed to be a recreation area as well as a source of water for the Southwestern Federated Power Cooperative. Construction of the lake did not start until 1950, however. The lake and recreation area were dedicated as a state park on September 20, 1953.

DESCRIPTION: The 990-acre Green Valley State Park has a 139-unit campground with showers, modern restrooms, and electrical hookups at 81 sites. The campground, a beach, and picnic grounds are located on the north central shore of the lake. Trails for hiking, cross-country skiing, and snowmobiling, as well as picnic areas, are located near the south end of the lake. Hiking trails are also located on the east side. On the northwestern edge of the lake is a wildlife refuge. The refuge is closed to the public from mid-September until mid-December.

The park also has a 1½-mile nature trail along the southwest shore of the lake—the Lake View Nature Trail. Requiring about one and a half hours of walking, the trail takes people through a gently rolling grassland habitat.

There are four boat ramps around the lake. Two ramps are located on the north shore, one of which is reserved for people using the campground. A third ramp is located on the east shore of the lake's western bend, and a fourth ramp is located on the south shore. Two handicapped-access fishing jetties are located on the lake: north of the dam on the west shore and near the boat ramp by the beach.

Green Valley State Park is located near the old Mormon Trail.

FLORA AND FAUNA: There are many types of trees, shrubs, and wildflowers. The park has many species of wildlife, including muskrats, deer, and beavers, as well as abundant migratory and native birds.

ACTIVITIES: In 1974 the 25-foot-deep lake was renovated and was later restocked with bluegills, crappies, channel catfish, largemouth bass, and northern bass. In the early 1980s, as part of an effort to increase water quality, a causeway was built across the northernmost arm of the lake. This

104

is a popular place for fishermen.

Boat motors must be operated at no-wake speeds on most of the lake, with the exception of the designated water-skiing area. Boating is not permitted from 10:30 P.M. until 4:00 A.M., and water-skiing is only permitted from 10:00 A.M. until sunset. Boats within the ski zone must maintain a no-wake speed before and after the permitted skiing hours.

Other activities offered include camping, swimming, bird-watching, picnicking, hiking, cross-country skiing, snowmobiling, and a nature trail.

ACKNOWLEDGMENT: James Lawson, park ranger, Green Valley State Park

FOR MORE INFORMATION:

Green Valley State Park. Des Moines: Iowa Department of Natural Resources.

Lake View Nature Trail. Des Moines: Iowa Department of Natural Resources.

National Park Service, U.S. Department of the Interior. Mormon Pioneer National Historic Trail. Washington, D.C.: Government Printing Office, 1981.

Holst State Forest

LOCATION: South edge of Fraser on a county road in Boone County

HISTORY: This forest was donated to the state in 1939 by B. P. Holst.

DESCRIPTION: The forest preserve covers 313 acres and lies upon glacial till with deep drainage cuts.

FLORA AND FAUNA: The forest is home to more than forty species of trees. There is also an abundance of birds, as many as forty-five species, and several kinds of mammals.

ACTIVITIES: Although not developed for recreational use, hunting for deer, squirrel, and rabbit is permitted. The forest is used for research, experimentation, nature study, management, and demonstration. Forestry students from Iowa State University frequently use the area as an outdoor classroom.

ACKNOWLEDGMENT: James Bulman, regional forester, Ames

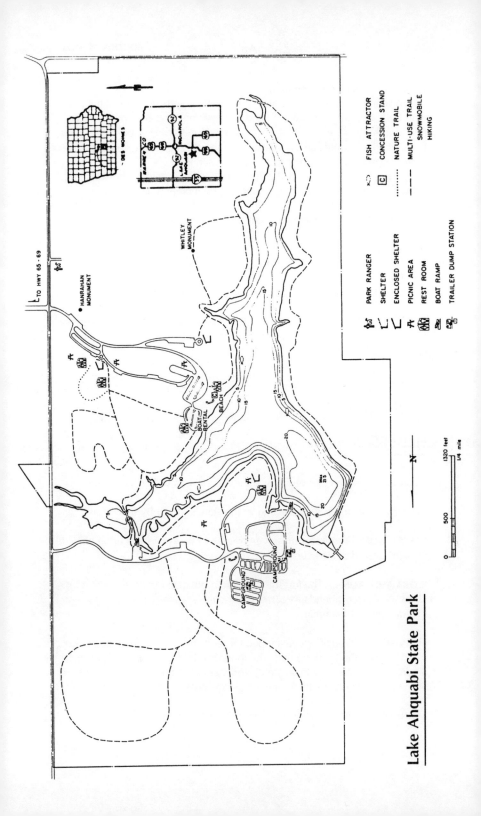

Lake Ahquabi State Park

Lake Ahquabi State Park

LOCATION: 5 miles south of Indianola on Highway 65/69, then west for ½ mile on Highway 349, in Warren County

ADDRESS: R.R. 1, Indianola, Iowa 50125

TELEPHONE: (515) 961-7101

HISTORY: Ahquabi to the Sac and Fox Indians meant "resting place." Although the Indians frequently visited this area, the name "Ahquabi" was the winning entry in a name-the-park contest in 1935.

In 1934, when the land was purchased by the city of Indianola, it was known as Oak Lake. The Civilian Conservation Corps began work on a lake, built several buildings out of sandstone, and established a nature trail between 1934 and 1935. Indianola deeded the land to the state, and on Sunday, May 29, 1936, the park was officially dedicated. The lake was opened to fishermen in 1937. Development of this state park received a strong recommendation from prominent Iowa conservationist J. N. "Ding" Darling.

A forested area of the park was dedicated as the Whitley Forest in 1938 by the Iowa Federation of Women's Clubs. They erected a monument honoring Mrs. Francis E. Whitley, who was a pioneer conservationist.

In 1966 the spillway was repaired, and Lake Ahquabi was renovated. Thirteen jetties were constructed along the shore for fishing. Some extend for 150 feet into the lake.

DESCRIPTION: Lake Ahquabi State Park covers 775 acres and has 9 miles of trails around the lake and throughout the park for hiking, snowmobiling, and cross-country skiing. The 114-acre artificial lake has a maximum depth of 21.5 feet near the dam. The Whitley monument is located to the south of the eastern picnic area.

The northern portion of the park has two boat docks, picnic areas, a shelter that is available for reservation, and the campground. The campground has showers, modern restrooms, and 161 campsites, 85 of which have electricity.

On the east side of the lake is a picnic area with a large playground, a supervised beach and bathhouse for swimmers (a small fee is charged), a nature trail, and a beautiful sandstone lodge on a hill that provides a scenic view of the lake. An open shelter, located in the picnic area, is also available for reservation. Also on the east shore is a concession stand offering fishing supplies, bait, and boat and motor rental, including paddleboats, canoes, and fishing boats. Any size boat motors may be operated at no-wake speeds.

The park lies in an area of glacial drift and windblown silt (loess) of the Kansan Glacial Stage, and has exposures of sandstone of the Floris Formation, Pennsylvanian Period. The sandstone is also exposed in an abandoned quarry.

The park has become very popular, attracting several hundred thousand visitors annually. Des Moines is only 20 miles away.

FLORA AND FAUNA: The park is heavily wooded. Oaks are common, and some have been estimated at five hundred years of age. More than 150 species of wildflowers occur here, and there is abundant wildlife, including a large deer herd.

ACTIVITIES: In the early 1980s, the lake was stocked with tiger muskies, walleyes, largemouth bass, channel catfish, bluegills, bullheads, sunfish, and crappies. Ice fishing is popular, as well as tobogganing down the hills and onto the frozen lake.

The Seven Bridges Interpretive Trail acquaints visitors with the park's plant and animal life. It requires about fifteen to thirty minutes of walking. Originally, the trail had seven bridges, but only two still remain.

Other activities offered in the park include bird-watching, sight-seeing, picnicking, swimming, a rental lodge, a concession stand, boating, hiking, camping, mushroom hunting, snowmobiling, and cross-country skiing.

ACKNOWLEDGMENT: Don Pudwill, park ranger, Lake Ahquabi State Park

FOR MORE INFORMATION:
Seven Bridges Interpretive Trail. Des Moines: Iowa Department of Natural Resources.

Lake Anita State Park

LOCATION: 1 mile south of Anita on Highway 148 in Cass County

ADDRESS: R.R. 1, Anita, Iowa 50020

TELEPHONE: (712) 762-3564

HISTORY: Lake Anita State Park is one of Iowa's newer state parks. It was dedicated in 1967. The artificial lake was formed by a dam on a branch of the Nishnabotna River, which runs along the northwestern part of the park.

DESCRIPTION: The park covers 942 acres and has a 182-acre artificial lake. It is located only 6 miles south of Interstate 80.

ACTIVITIES: A swimming beach and bathhouse are located in the central area of the park, opposite the dam. Several jetties were constructed along the shore of the lake for fishermen. Crappies, perch, tiger muskie, largemouth bass, bullheads, bluegills, and channel catfish are present. A concession stand sells fishing supplies and snacks, and rents boats and boat motors. Any size boat motors may be operated at no-wake speeds. The park also offers mushroom hunting, a nature trail, and a playground.

The park's picnic areas have a total of eight open shelters, which may be reserved. A golf course is located near the park. Snowmobiling is allowed in the winter. There is a 150-site campground with electricity at 75 sites, modern restrooms, and showers. Some of the sites also feature water hookups. Due to the park's location near busy Interstate 80, the campground receives a lot of use.

ACKNOWLEDGMENT: Larry Van Horn, park ranger, Lake Anita State Park

FOR MORE INFORMATION:
Lake Anita Conservation Trail. Des Moines: Iowa Department of Natural Resources.
Lake Anita State Park. Des Moines: Iowa Department of Natural Resources.
Welcome to Anita A Whale of a Town. Anita: Anita Chamber of Commerce.

Lake Manawa State Park

LOCATION: Southern edge of Council Bluffs off Highway 192 (south expressway) in Pottawattamie County

ADDRESS: Council Bluffs, Iowa 51501

TELEPHONE: (712) 336-0220

HISTORY: Lake Manawa is one of many oxbow lakes formed by changes in

109

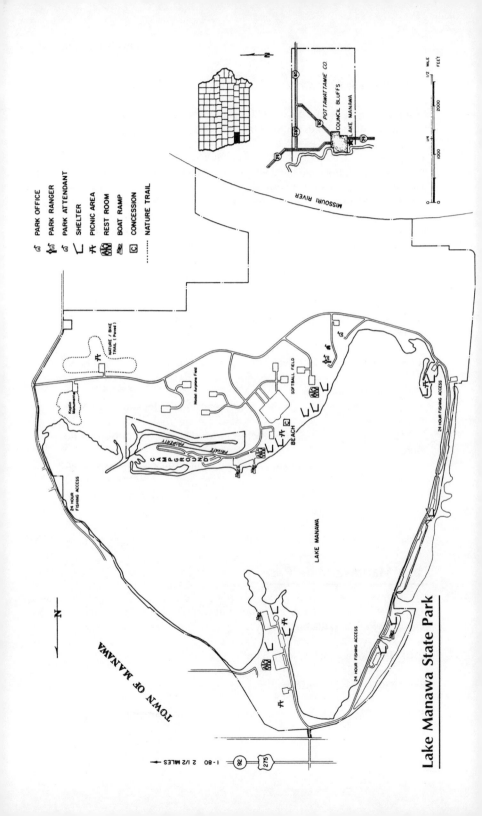

Lake Manawa State Park

Legend

- ⌂ PARK OFFICE
- PARK RANGER
- ⌂ PARK ATTENDANT
- SHELTER
- PICNIC AREA
- REST ROOM
- BOAT RAMP
- CONCESSION
- ········ NATURE TRAIL

MISSOURI RIVER

POTTAWATTAMIE CO.

COUNCIL BLUFFS

LAKE MANAWA

1/4   1/2 MILE

1000   2000 FEET

0

N

TOWN OF MANAWA

I-80 2 1/2 MILES

275

LAKE MANAWA

CAMPGROUND

PRIVATE PROPERTY

CONCORD

BEACH

SOFTBALL FIELD

Model Airplane Field

Kaplan Monument

NATURE / BIKE TRAIL (Paved)

24 HOUR FISHING ACCESS

24 HOUR FISHING ACCESS

24 HOUR FISHING ACCESS

the course of the Missouri River. This lake was probably formed around 1818 when a flood caused the river to shift, cutting off the lake. Originally known as "Cutoff Lake," the lake was later renamed in honor of Chief Manawa of the Pottawattamie Indians.

The area was a very popular recreation site around the turn of the century. However, a series of disasters—including two major fires, tornadoes, and the collapse of part of the dance hall into the lake—contributed to a decline in the area's popularity.

The lake itself had also been plagued with problems. Situated on the Missouri River floodplain, the lake received large amounts of silt from nearly annual river floods. By 1935 the lake had an average depth of only 4 feet. The lake was dredged, but this was only a temporary solution. In the 1930s, equipment was installed to pump water into the lake from the Missouri River and Misquito Creek. By the 1970s, it became evident that additional dredging was needed. In 1983–84, at a cost of more than $2.5 million, the lake was dredged again and levees were constructed. This is expected to extend the life of the lake by a century.

DESCRIPTION: The lake is adjacent to the old Mormon Trail and is situated between Misquito Creek on the east and Indian Creek on the west. Twenty-four–hour fishing accesses are located on the northwest, southwest, and southeast shores of the 660-acre lake.

Lake Manawa lies in the Missouri River flyway, which is used by migratory birds. The river runs along the southern edge of the park. Lake Manawa is the number one recreational lake in the Omaha–Council Bluffs area.

The peninsula on the north shore has picnic areas and a boat ramp. This area is now managed by the city of Council Bluffs. Other picnic grounds, a boat access, a supervised beach, and a modern campground may be found along the south shore.

A surfaced nature trail is located in the southeast corner of the park. Only a mile south of Interstates 80 and 29, the 1,530-acre park receives many hundreds of thousands of visitors annually.

FLORA: One of the most notable plants found on the lake is the American lotus.

ACTIVITIES: Lake Manawa State Park has a 68-site campground with modern shower facilities; 35 of the sites have electrical hookups. The park also offers picnicking at a number of shelters that may be reserved, supervised swimming, boat rental, bird-watching, a nature trail, water-skiing, mushroom hunting, a bicycle trail, and snowmobiling. Any size boat motors may be operated on Lake Manawa.

111

ACKNOWLEDGMENT: Donald DeLong, park ranger, Lake Manawa State Park

FOR MORE INFORMATION:
Lake Manawa State Park. Des Moines: Iowa Department of Natural Resources.
National Park Service, U.S. Department of the Interior. *Mormon Pioneer National Historic Trail.* Washington, D.C.: Government Printing Office, 1981.

Lake of Three Fires State Park

LOCATION: 3 miles northeast of Bedford on Highway 49 in Taylor County

ADDRESS: R.R. 4, Bedford, Iowa 50833

TELEPHONE: (712) 523-2700

HISTORY: Before the first settlers arrived, according to legend, this area was the scene of large Indian council meetings. Messengers informed other Indian nations of future meetings and their approximate locations. The exact locations of the meetings were told by smoke signals from three fires on a hill. The meetings were probably held in the valley, which is now flooded by the lake. The name "Lake of Three Fires" was officially approved by the Iowa Conservation Commission in 1937. Construction of the lake and park began in 1935, and it was officially opened to the public in March 1938. Development was done by the Civilian Conservation Corps and included a stone and wood shelter and six cabins.

In 1980 the lake was drained. Jetties for fishing were built along the shore. The carp were chemically killed off, and the lake was restocked with bass, bluegills, crappies, bullheads, channel catfish, and tiger muskies.

DESCRIPTION: The 85-acre lake has a maximum depth of 17 feet south of the dam, which is 1 mile long and ½ mile wide. The park itself covers 691 acres.

The east side of the lake has a popular campground, picnic areas, a swimming beach, hiking trails, a boat ramp, and six cabins that can be rented. The west side of the lake has bridle and snowmobile trails. On the lake, only electric boat motors are permitted.

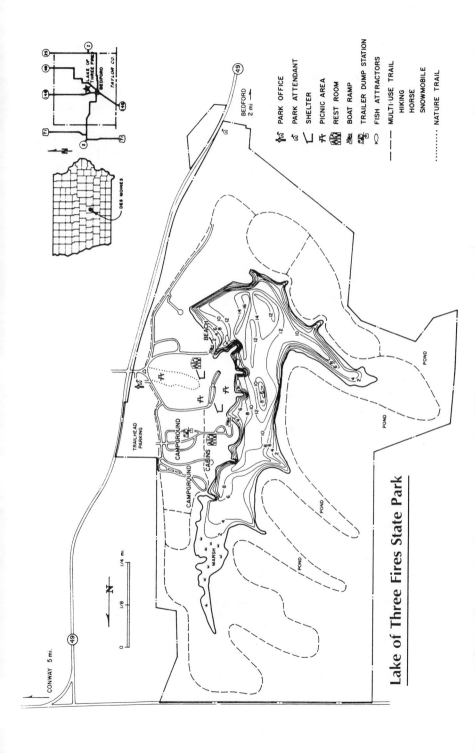

Lake of Three Fires State Park

PARK OFFICE
PARK ATTENDANT
SHELTER
PICNIC AREA
REST ROOM
BOAT RAMP
TRAILER DUMP STATION
FISH ATTRACTORS
MULTI-USE TRAIL
HIKING
HORSE
SNOWMOBILE
NATURE TRAIL

BEDFORD 2 mi.

CONWAY 5 mi.

BEACH
MARSH
CABINS
CAMPGROUND
CAMPGROUND
TRAILHEAD PARKING
POND

LAKE OF THREE FIRES
BEDFORD
TAYLOR CO.

DES MOINES

N

0   1/8   1/4 mi.

FLORA AND FAUNA: The thickly wooded hills of the park are primarily made up of oaks, many of which are quite old. The park is the home for many species of wildlife as well.

ACTIVITIES: The campground has a total of 112 sites with modern restrooms and showers. Thirty of the sites are equipped with electricity. There are two shelters that may be reserved and six cabins available on a rental basis. Other popular activities in the park include bird-watching, photography, mushroom hunting, fishing, picnicking, swimming, hiking, bridle trails, and snowmobiling. To enjoy the park at its best, the staff recommends a summer visit.

ACKNOWLEDGMENT: Harry Hunter, park ranger, Lake of Three Fires State Park

FOR MORE INFORMATION:
> *Bedford Times-Press.* Annual "Lake of Three Fires" edition. 1986.
> *Lake of Three Fires.* Des Moines: Iowa Department of Natural Resources.

Ledges State Park

LOCATION: 6 miles south of Boone on Highway 164 in Boone County

ADDRESS: Madrid, Iowa 50156

TELEPHONE: (515) 432-1852

HISTORY: The site of the present-day Ledges State Park was once a popular area for powwows and council meetings by the Sioux and later the Sac and Fox (Mesquakie). A bluff overlooking the Des Moines River served as a lookout site during the meetings and became known as "Sentinel Rock."

In 1921 the land was acquired by the state, and on November 9, 1924, Ledges State Park was officially dedicated. Early development of the park was done in the 1930s by the Civilian Conservation Corps. Since then, Ledges has become one of the most popular recreation areas in central Iowa.

DESCRIPTION: Ledges State Park is noted for its natural beauty and diver-

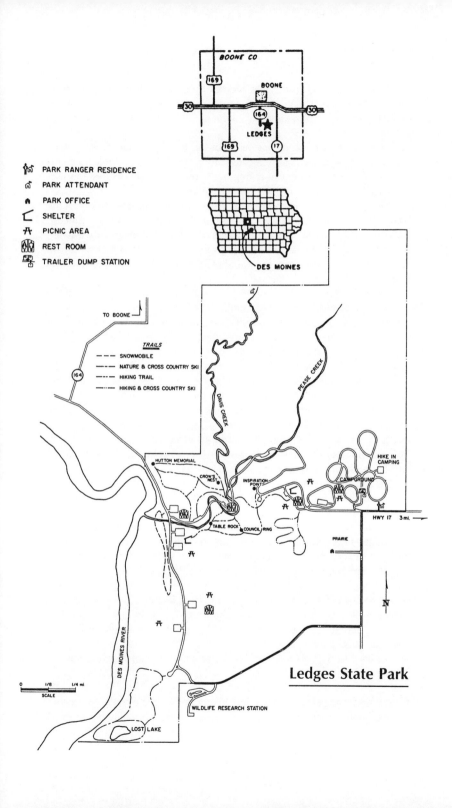

PARK RANGER RESIDENCE

PARK ATTENDANT

PARK OFFICE

SHELTER

PICNIC AREA

REST ROOM

TRAILER DUMP STATION

BOONE CO

BOONE

LEDGES

DES MOINES

TO BOONE

TRAILS

SNOWMOBILE

NATURE & CROSS COUNTRY SKI

HIKING TRAIL

HIKING & CROSS COUNTRY SKI

DAVIS CREEK

PEASE CREEK

HUTTON MEMORIAL

CROW'S NEST

INSPIRATION POINT

HIKE IN CAMPING

CAMPGROUND

TABLE ROCK

COUNCIL RING

HWY 17   3 mi.

PRAIRIE

N

DES MOINES RIVER

Ledges State Park

0   1/8   1/4 mi
SCALE

WILDLIFE RESEARCH STATION

LOST LAKE

sity. The park rises from the Des Moines River and features river bottom, rugged woodlands, stream, and upland-prairie habitats. The park features an excellent system of hiking trails, which link its natural and recreational features.

The "ledges" are sandstone bluffs of the Pennsylvanian Period, Floris Formation. They are primarily located along Pea's Creek and reach heights of up to 75 feet. A system of hiking trails runs above the ledges and provides spectacular views of the beautiful valley below.

There are two creeks in the park. Davis Creek enters the park from the north. Pea's Creek, named after an early settler, enters from the northeast. The creeks meet in the central area of the park and then meander westward to the Des Moines River. On its way to the river, the crystal clear stream crosses the canyon roadway in several places. The Des Moines River flows along the western part of the park.

Near the river, in the northwest corner of the park, is the Hutton Memorial, honoring Murray Lee Hutton (1886–1941). Hutton was a strong believer in conservation and authored several articles on the topic. In 1935 he was named the first director of the Iowa Conservation Commission.

In the southwestern part of the park is Lost Lake; Katina Pond and Katina Falls, located to the north of the lake; Sentinel Rock, overlooking the river; and River Edge Woods, situated between Lost Lake and Katina Pond. There is a hiking trail in this area. Also in the southern area of the park are Deer Edge Woods and Walking Fern Hollow. The eastern area has a re-established prairie, the Oak Woods picnic area, and the modern campground that features two shower buildings and 40 electrically equipped sites, as well as a number of "walk-in" campsites. The western area has a snowmobile trail, picnic grounds, and a CCC shelter. Hiking trails connect the eastern and western areas.

Efforts have been under way since 1980 to improve the park's trails. Other improvements have been made to the park's facilities to meet demands put upon them by the increasing popularity of the park. These include the new campground and restroom facilities. The park attracts hundreds of thousands of visitors annually and in all seasons. An estimated 600,000 people live within an hour's drive of Ledges.

FLORA AND FAUNA: Some of the largest trees in Iowa grow in the park. Ledges State Park also has a wide abundance of wildflowers and other plants, including such rare species as closed gentian, walking fern, pussytoes, and showy orchis.

At least forty-five species of birds and many species of mammals can be found here.

ACTIVITIES: Ledges State Park offers hiking trails, nature trails, picnicking, a playground, stream fishing, boating, open shelters that may be reserved,

116

scenic overlooks, snowmobiling, cross-country skiing, bird-watching, and photography. The park's 81-site campground is equipped with electrical hookups, modern restrooms, and showers.

ACKNOWLEDGMENTS: Dick Kaduce, park ranger, Ledges State Park
   Staff at the State Archives

FOR MORE INFORMATION:
   Ledges State Park. Des Moines: Iowa Department of Natural Resources.
   Ledges State Park Newsletter. Des Moines: Iowa Department of Natural Resources, annual.

Lennon Mills State Park

LOCATION: Southwest edge of Panora on a county road in Guthrie County

ADDRESS: Guthrie County Conservation Board, Guthrie Center, Iowa 50115

TELEPHONE: (515) 755-3061 (Guthrie County Conservation Board)

HISTORY: A historical marker was placed here at the site of the Panora Woolen Mill, built by James and John Clive in 1861–62 and later operated as a flour mill until 1940. In 1959 it was finally demolished.

DESCRIPTION: Lennon Mills State Park is a 21-acre site along the Middle Raccoon River. Adjacent to the park is the 285-acre Lennon Mills Wildlife Area. With timber and upland habitats, the area offers squirrel, rabbit, deer, quail, and pheasant hunting.

ACTIVITIES: The park has a campground with electrical hookups, picnic grounds, and hiking trails, and there is fishing in the river. Hunting is permitted nearby.

Lewis and Clark State Park

LOCATION: 3 miles west of Onawa on Highway 175, then north on Highway 324, in Monona County

ADDRESS: Onawa, Iowa 51040

TELEPHONE: (712) 423-2829

HISTORY: Lewis and Clark State Park was named in honor of the explorers Captain Meriwether Lewis and Lieutenant William Clark. Commissioned by President Thomas Jefferson, the two men and an expedition force of about thirty men began their exploration of the Missouri River from Wood River, near St. Louis, on May 21, 1804. In early August of that year, the expedition spent several days along the east shore of the present-day Blue Lake, which was then part of the river channel. The men reported several sand dunes, river sandbars, and a few cottonwood trees.

A granite monument to Lewis and Clark was placed at the park entrance, courtesy of the Daughters of the American Revolution. Blue Lake, an oxbow, was formed in the mid-1800s by a westward shift in the Missouri River due to flooding.

Originally covering 286 acres, Lewis and Clark State Park was officially dedicated in August 1924. Between that year and the start of World War II, numerous projects and improvements were instigated. One of the projects was a lodge built with Pennsylvanian-age fossiliferous limestone and black chert.

Like many oxbow lakes along the Missouri River, Blue Lake has had problems with siltation and a dropping water level. In the early 1950s, the lake was dredged and pumps were installed to pump water into the lake from a well. Despite these problems, the lake remains a popular site. Additional dredging and installation of new pumps were done in 1980.

DESCRIPTION: The park, comprising 176 heavily wooded acres on the Missouri River floodplain, is located on the west shore of the lake, with a rental lodge (available May through October) located in the south central part of the park. The lake covers 230 acres and has a maximum depth of 10 feet. The park's modern 35-acre campground is located along the lakeshore. It features eighty-one sites, many of which are located along the shore. All feature electrical hookups. A beautifully shaded picnic area is located along the southwest shore. Several hiking and nature trails can be found to the west of the campground.

Bordering the park on the west is 865 acres of marsh, shallow lake, and upland habitats where waterfowl, pheasant, and rabbit hunting are

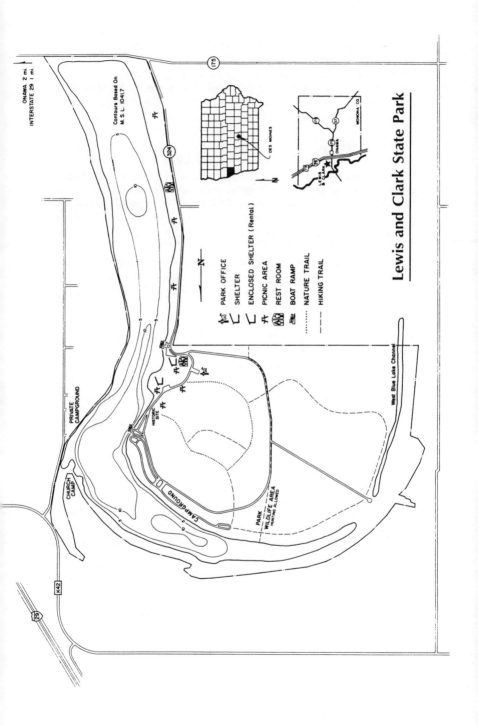

Lewis and Clark State Park

ONAWA 2 mi.
INTERSTATE 29 1 mi.

Contours Based On
M. S. L. 1041.7

PRIVATE CAMPGROUND

CHURCH CAMP

CAMPGROUND

HISTORIC SITE

PARK WILDLIFE AREA
HUNTING ALLOWED

West Blue Lake Channel

DES MOINES

MONONA CO.

ONAWA

LEWIS & CLARK

-N-

𝌀 PARK OFFICE

⌐ SHELTER

⌐ ENCLOSED SHELTER (Rental)

⚲ PICNIC AREA

REST ROOM

BOAT RAMP

.... NATURE TRAIL

- - - - HIKING TRAIL

permitted. This is the Blue Lake Wildlife Management Area.

FLORA AND FAUNA: The park has abundant mammals, birds, amphibians, trees, shrubs, wildflowers, and prairie grasses. Some of the cottonwood trees here were present during Lewis and Clark's day. One of these still grows between the lodge and the beach. It is one of the park's focal points.

ACTIVITIES: The park offers fishing, swimming, water-skiing, two boat ramps, snowmobiling, a rental lodge, ice-skating, picnicking, camping (electricity, modern restrooms, showers), hiking, and nature trails. There is no restriction on the size of boat motors. Fish that are present include walleyes, largemouth bass, northern pike, bluegills, crappies, and channel catfish. Hunting is permitted in the adjacent wildlife management area. There is also an amphitheater in the park where nature films are shown during the summer.

The park has a 1-mile-long nature trail, the "Early Explorer Trail." With twenty-nine stops, the trail requires about an hour to complete.

In early summer, the park is the scene of the Onawa–Lewis and Clark Festival, a special event featuring attractions for all ages. A highlight of the park is the 55-foot authentic replica of Lewis and Clark's keelboat, "Discovery." Work began on the boat in 1985; it was built with oak lumber from Yellow River State Forest. Its designer, Butch Bouvier of Council Bluffs, other area volunteers, and park staff worked on the boat's construction for several years. The boat is truly unique and has been featured in the *Smithsonian Magazine*.

ACKNOWLEDGMENT: Ron Williams, park ranger, Lewis and Clark State Park

FOR MORE INFORMATION:
Early Explorer Trail, Lewis and Clark State Park. Des Moines: Iowa Department of Natural Resources.
Lewis and Clark State Park. Des Moines: Iowa Department of Natural Resources.
Monona County History. Onawa: Monona County Historical Society, 1981.

Margo Frankel Woods State Park

LOCATION: 2 miles north of Des Moines on Highway 415 in Polk County

ADDRESS: Big Creek State Park, R.R. 1, Polk City, Iowa 50226

TELEPHONE: (515) 984-6473 (Big Creek State Park)

HISTORY: The land comprising Margo Frankel Woods State Park was used by Sac and Fox Indians up until 1845 when they moved west to the Missouri River and sold the land to the federal government. Captain Allen of Fort Des Moines was placed in charge of issuing permits to settlers who wished to move here. In exchange for the permits, the settlers were asked to help supply the fort, which was located at Raccoon Forks (now Des Moines).

The land, previously known as Saylor Woods (after John B. and John P. Saylor, who settled here in the 1840s), was purchased by the Greater Des Moines Committee in 1945. They, in turn, donated it to the state for the purpose of developing a state park. The committee believed that such a park would become quite popular since it was so close to Des Moines. The state renamed the land after Mrs. Margo Frankel, a supporter of, and leader in, conservation. Mr. Henry Frankel donated 12 acres of woods on a hill adjacent to the park on the west and 20 acres of thick woods and ravines on the east side of the park. These were incorporated into the state park.

DESCRIPTION: The park covers a total of 136 acres. The western area across Highway 415 has a bridle trail. The eastern area has two picnic areas, each with a shelter and nonmodern restroom. Playground equipment is located in the south picnic area. The Camp Sunnyside Sidewalk is located in the northeastern part. A hiking trail connects the northern and southern areas of the park.

The park is located only a few miles north of Interstate 80 and 3 miles west of Interstate 35.

ACTIVITIES: The park offers nature study, sight-seeing, a bridle trail, hiking, and picnicking.

ACKNOWLEDGMENT: Rod Slings, park ranger, Big Creek State Park

FOR MORE INFORMATION:
Margo Frankel Woods State Park. Des Moines: Iowa Department of Natural Resources.

Nine Eagles State Park

LOCATION: 6 miles southeast of Davis City on County Road J-66 in Decatur County

ADDRESS: Davis City, Iowa 50065

TELEPHONE: (515) 442-2855

HISTORY: Forty acres in the southwestern part of Nine Eagles State Park were originally part of the Allen Scott farm. Scott was one of the first settlers here in 1839.

The name "Nine Eagles" was given to the first post office in the county. Legend has it that a prominent early family in the area had nine lively children who were known locally as the "nine eagles."

In the summer of 1949, local citizens purchased the property at $10 an acre and donated it to the state, along with $2,000 to help develop a state park. A dam was completed in the 1950s at a cost of $237,600.

DESCRIPTION: The park has a total of one hundred campsites. Electricity at forty-six sites, modern restrooms, and showers are available. Camping is allowed in two locations in the eastern part of the 1,100-acre park. On the northeast shore of the lake is a swimming beach. To the east of the beach are boat docks and a boat ramp. Only rowboats and boats with electric motors are permitted on the lake. Many scenic areas can be found in the western part of the park and near the northeast shore of the lake. Bridle trails are located in the northern part of the park. Hiking and snowmobile trails are located throughout the park.

FLORA AND FAUNA: Most of the park is heavily wooded with oak trees, which provide colorful autumn scenes. The park has abundant plant and animal life. Deer and waterfowl are particularly noteworthy.

ACTIVITIES: Largemouth bass, channel catfish, bluegills, northern pike, sunfish, and crappies are present for fishermen. The park also offers camping, bird-watching, swimming, scenic views, bridle trails, picnicking, hiking, and snowmobiling.

ACKNOWLEDGMENTS: Park ranger, Nine Eagles State Park
    Staff at the State Archives

FOR MORE INFORMATION:
    Nine Eagles State Park. Des Moines: Iowa Department of Natural Resources.

Pammel State Park

LOCATION: 2 miles west of Winterset on Highway 92, then south for 3 miles on Highway 322, in Madison County

ADDRESS: Madison County Conservation Board, Box 129, Winterset, Iowa 50273

TELEPHONE: (515) 462-3536 (Madison County Conservation Board)

HISTORY: A tunnel was dug by hand through shale beneath a limestone ridge here. A dam was then constructed on the Middle River to force water to flow through the tunnel to a flour mill and sawmill on the east side of the ridge. The dam, tunnel, and mill were built over a three-year period by John Harmon and his sons in the late 1850s. In 1904 the mill was abandoned and, in 1913, demolished. A plaque commemorating the mill is located at the entrance to the park.

Originally known as the "Devil's Backbone," the land was acquired by the state in 1923. The name was changed to avoid confusion with Backbone State Park in Delaware County. The park was named in honor of Dr. Louis H. Pammel, a noted botanist at Iowa State College (now Iowa State University) and a strong supporter of conservation.

DESCRIPTION: The 281-acre Pammel State Park has the state's only automobile tunnel, located in the northern part of the park. Pammel is a heavily wooded park with rugged topography. There are 2 miles of hiking trails at Pammel that provide visitors an excellent look at the park's natural beauty. A nature trail and a snowmobile trail are located in the western part.

A rustic lodge, built by the CCC in the 1930s, is located southwest of the Middle River ford and can be rented. An open shelter with fireplace (which may be reserved) is located at the south end of the ridge near the campground. The thirty-two–site campground lacks electricity and modern restrooms. In this area, the limestone ridge (Bethany Falls Member, Swope Formation, Pennsylvanian Period) is 140 feet high.

The Middle River flows along the west side of the ridge and then curves and flows along the east side. The river may be canoed except in dry periods. Below the river ford to the west of the tunnel is a popular fishing hole in the river. Catfish, bullheads, carp, and bluegills can be caught. The road crosses the Middle River at the ford west of the tunnel, but during winter or high water, the crossing may be closed.

In late 1989, the park was transferred to the Madison County Conservation Board.

FLORA AND FAUNA: The park has one of the widest varieties of understory

123

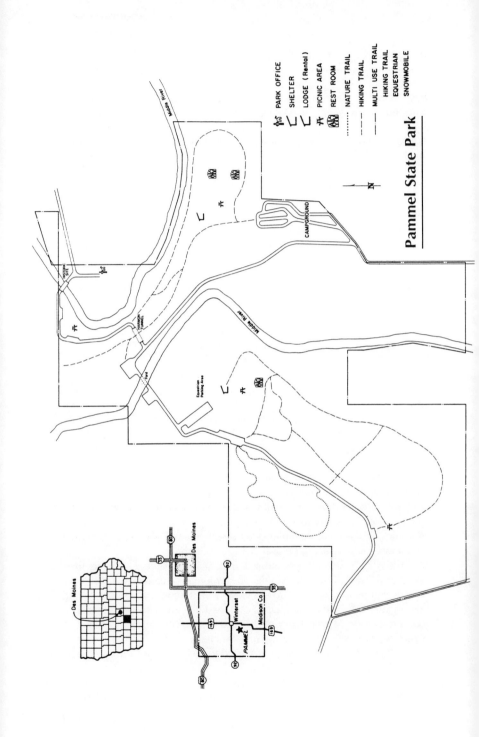

Pammel State Park

PARK OFFICE
SHELTER
LODGE (Rental)
PICNIC AREA
REST ROOM
·········· NATURE TRAIL
- - - - HIKING TRAIL
— - — MULTI USE TRAIL
HIKING TRAIL
EQUESTRIAN
SNOWMOBILE

N

CAMPGROUND

Equestrian
Parking Area

Middle River

HISTORIC
SITE

TUNNEL

Ford

Middle River

Des Moines

Des Moines

Des Moines

Winterset

Madison Co

PAMMEL

plant life in the state and a wide variety of animals and birds. There are various trees and shrubs, including several oaks dating as far back as the 1630s.

ACTIVITIES: Swimming and wading are allowed in the river. The park also offers a scenic view from the top of the ridge, fishing, a nature trail, canoeing, camping, a museum, mushroom hunting, hiking, snowmobiling, cross-country skiing, and picnicking. The campground is open all year but may be inaccessible in the winter.

ACKNOWLEDGMENT: Kirk Mathis, park ranger, Pammel State Park

FOR MORE INFORMATION:
Pammel State Park. Des Moines: Iowa Department of Natural Resources.

Pilot Mound State Forest

LOCATION: ½ mile south of Pilot Mound on a county road in Boone County

HISTORY: The land was donated to the state in 1939 by B. P. Holst. The town of Pilot Mound at one time placed its water supply here. The land is elevated above the surrounding terrain and serves as a natural water tower.

DESCRIPTION: The Pilot Mound State Forest is 33 acres of forest resting on glacial till near the Des Moines River. It is sparse in flora and fauna but is used for study and research in the maintenance of forest growth. The forest has not been developed for recreational use or for timber use. To the southeast is the Holst State Forest.

ACTIVITIES: Picnicking, walking, and hunting are permitted.

ACKNOWLEDGMENT: James Bulman, regional forester, Ames

Prairie Rose State Park

LOCATION: 6 miles east of Harlan on Highway 44, then south for 3 miles on County Road M-47, in Shelby County

ADDRESS: R.R. 4, Harlan, Iowa 51537

TELEPHONE: (712) 773-2701

HISTORY: Prairie Rose was the name of a town founded in 1895, which was so named because of the abundance of prairie roses in the area. Nothing remains of the town today, which was located 1 mile east and ½ mile south of the park entrance.

Because there was no state park in the area, $389,000 was allocated in the late 1940s to develop a park and lake. However, not until 1952 was this site finally chosen out of a field of sixteen and the purchase of the land begun. The lake and park were completed and opened to the public in 1962. More than twenty-one thousand trees were planted on the land.

Renovation and restocking of the lake were carried out in the early 1980s. With special watershed-improvement work and the cooperation of local farmers, erosion and siltation buildup have been kept at a minimum, and lake-water quality has been improved.

DESCRIPTION: The lake covers 204 acres with a maximum depth of 26 feet. The long, narrow lake is located in the center of the park and offers bass, bullhead, bluegill, catfish, crappie, and carp fishing.

Boat ramps are located on the south and northeast shores. Any size boat motors may be operated at no-wake speeds. Also located near the south shore are the campground and a picnic area with shelter (which may be reserved). The campground has 61 sites with modern restrooms, showers, electricity, and scenic views of the lake.

Along the north central shore is another picnic area with shelter (which may be reserved) that affords scenic views of the lake and hills of loess (windblown silt deposited during glacial times). Also in the vicinity is an unsupervised beach for swimmers.

The park is located only 7½ miles north of the Interstate 80 Walnut exit.

ACTIVITIES: Cross-country skiing, ice-skating, and sledding are popular winter activities here. Snowmobiling and iceboating are also permitted. Other activities offered include camping, picnicking, fishing, group camping, scenic views, and swimming.

ACKNOWLEDGMENT: Robert Glenn, park ranger, Prairie Rose State Park

FOR MORE INFORMATION:
Prairie Rose State Park. Des Moines: Iowa Department of Natural Resources.

Preparation Canyon State Park

LOCATION: 2 miles south of Moorhead on Highway 183, then west for 3 miles on County Road E-60, in Monona County

ADDRESS: Lewis and Clark State Park, Onawa, Iowa 51040

TELEPHONE: (712) 423-2829 (Lewis and Clark State Park)

HISTORY: In 1853 Charles Thompson, known as "Father Ephraim," led about fifty families away from the main caravan following the Mormon Trail and went to Kanesville, now known as Council Bluffs. He claimed that this was the wish of a spirit known as "Baneemy." From there, they searched for an area in which to settle and prepare themselves for the "life beyond." That same year, they found a valley that the Indians called Monona or "peaceful valley," and founded the town of Preparation.

In 1934 the state purchased 82 acres in the area from Martha and Walter Perrin, who were descendants of one of the original families here. In 1969 Martha sold an additional 157 acres to the state and later also sold the Perrin homestead. The land included the old townsite of Preparation.

DESCRIPTION: Today the 344-acre park has several streams and springs. The canyon has been largely untouched by man and has ridges along the north, south, and west. Camping is not permitted in the park. There are areas for picnicking, and the eastern two-thirds of the park has hiking and cross-country skiing trails. A nature study area is also located in the eastern part. The northwestern portion of the park offers scenic views of loess hills and the Missouri River floodplain.

Preparation Canyon is located in the beautiful loess hills, formed by windblown soil thousands of years ago. The rugged loess hills are located only along the Missouri River in Missouri and Iowa. The only similar deposits are found in China!

FLORA AND FAUNA: The park has an abundance of trees and wildflowers. There is abundant wildlife also, including white-tailed deer and wild turkey.

ACTIVITIES: Offered here are picnicking, hiking, nature study, cross-country skiing, and scenic views.

ACKNOWLEDGMENT: Ron Williams, park ranger, Lewis and Clark State Park

FOR MORE INFORMATION:
 Preparation Canyon State Park. Des Moines: Iowa Department of Natural Resources.

Sheeder Prairie State Preserve

LOCATION: 5 miles west of Guthrie Center off Highway 44 in Guthrie County

HISTORY: The prairie was purchased in 1961 from Oscar Sheeder by the state. His father was the original homesteader. It was dedicated as a state preserve in 1968.

DESCRIPTION: The preserve is a 25-acre native prairie. Its soil is comprised of loess and glacial till of the Kansas Glacial Stage, Pleistocene Epoch. An old Indian trail can still be seen here.

FLORA: Comprising upland prairie and mesic prairie, the preserve is home to 180 species of plants, including many wildflowers and prairie grasses.

ACTIVITIES: The preserve offers nature study.

Springbrook State Park

LOCATION: 7 miles north of Guthrie Center on Highway 25, then 1 mile east on Highway 384, in Guthrie County

ADDRESS: R.R. 1, Box 49, Guthrie Center, Iowa 50015

TELEPHONE: (515) 747-3591

HISTORY: Originally known as "King's Park," the land was acquired in 1926 from the King family. It was later named after a spring-fed creek in the area. A dam was built across Springbrook Creek to form an artificial lake. Most of the development in the park was done by the Civilian Conservation Corps in the 1930s.

DESCRIPTION: The park covers 794 acres and has a 16-acre artificial lake. Boat ramps are located on both the lake and the Raccoon River. Only electric boat motors are permitted on the lake.

Near the center of the park, south of the lake, is a 200-site campground with electricity at 55 sites, showers, and modern restrooms. The group camp area is also located here and has nine cabins, each of which can accommodate fourteen people. Kitchen, dining, shower, and meeting facilities are located here. It originally served as the group camp for the CCC workers.

The lake is located in the northwestern part of the park and is ringed by a nature trail. Also in the northwestern part are six family cabins available for rental. A supervised beach for swimmers is present, with a concession stand offering snacks, fishing supplies, and boat rental.

A snowmobile trail is located in the western area of the park and around the lake. There is also a mile-long interpretive trail that runs from the dam to the concession stand. Parts of the park offer scenic views, and Indian mounds can be found in one of the picnic areas.

The park has exposures of sandstone of the Nishnabotna Member, Dakota Formation, which was deposited during the Cretaceous Period. There are also glacial till and boulders left by a glacier during the Wisconsin Glacial Stage. The melting glacier cut a gorge through here that is up to 100 feet deep.

In 1970 the Iowa Conservation Education Center was opened in the park. The center is unique in the state and was designated as a National Environmental Education landmark by the National Park Service three years later.

FLORA AND FAUNA: The park is heavily wooded and has a wide variety of

129

plants and animals, including many species of birds and about two hundred deer. Wild turkey and white-tailed deer may be seen from roads and trails. Also within the park is a 6-foot-high dam built by beavers.

ACTIVITIES: The park offers picnicking, cross-country skiing, hiking, ice fishing, snowmobiling, a nature trail, boating, a concession stand, a group camp, rental cabins, camping, scenic views, supervised swimming, a playground, and fishing (crappies, largemouth bass, bluegills, bullheads, catfish).

The education center offers weekend workshops for educators and students on nature, natural resources, and the work of the Department of Natural Resources. Week-long workshops for educators are also offered and are the cooperative efforts of several state agencies.

During the summer, the park sponsors GASP!, the Great Annual Springbrook Park bicycle ride.

ACKNOWLEDGMENT: Scott Zager, park attendant, Springbrook State Park

FOR MORE INFORMATION:
Springbrook State Park. Des Moines: Iowa Department of Natural Resources.

Spring Lake State Park

LOCATION: 2 miles west of Grand Junction on Highway 30, then 2 miles north on County Road P-33, in Greene County

ADDRESS: Greene County Conservation Board, Jefferson, Iowa 50129

TELEPHONE: (515) 386-3849 (Greene County Conservation Board)

HISTORY: In the late 1860s, the Northwestern Railroad opened up a gravel pit here along West Buttrick Creek. The pit later became flooded by exceptionally clear springwater. In 1925 the pond was the site of a private resort.

In 1969 the Greene County Conservation Board was granted a long-term management agreement to the park and the lake. Badly needed improvements were then carried out.

DESCRIPTION: The lake covers 50 acres and the park covers 240 acres. The park is heavily used in the summer.

ACTIVITIES: Spring Lake State Park offers camping with electrical hookups, picnicking, hiking, swimming, fishing, a boat ramp (electric motors only), snowmobiling, a baseball diamond, and facilities for the handicapped. The picnic area is shaded by cottonwood trees.

ACKNOWLEDGMENT: Staff at the Jefferson Public Library

Swan Lake State Park

LOCATION: 2 miles south of Carroll on Highway 71, then 1 mile east on a county road, in Carroll County

ADDRESS: Carroll County Conservation Board, Carroll, Iowa 51401

TELEPHONE: (712) 792-4614

HISTORY: Before the turn of the century, Swan Lake was nearly 20 feet deep. In the early 1900s, local farmers attempted to drain the lake for use as farmland. Although they successfully drained it, they could not keep the land dry because of springs in the area. The lake became overgrown with weeds.

The state acquired the first 229 acres of the park in 1933–34, and Works Progress Administration members developed Swan Lake State Park. A dam was constructed to raise the lake's water level. The park was officially dedicated in 1937. However, problems with vegetation growth continued to plague Swan Lake, and the area lost its popularity.

In 1959 the Carroll County Conservation Board was granted a management agreement to the park. Since then, there have been major renovations to the lake and the park's facilities.

DESCRIPTION: Swan Lake State Park comprises 508 acres and a 134-acre artificial lake. There is a 200-site campground on the south shore of the lake with modern restrooms and showers. One hundred of the sites are equipped with electricity. The spring-fed lake has been stocked with channel catfish, crappies, bullheads, largemouth bass, and northern pike. A boat ramp is located on the south shore. Any size boat motors may be operated at no-wake speeds.

Also on the south side, to the east of the campground, is a concession stand where boats can be rented and refreshments, groceries, and fishing supplies are available. The stand is open from Memorial Day weekend through the Labor Day weekend.

The lake was dredged between 1982 and 1985 to a depth of 13 feet in order to prevent winter fish kills and to improve boating opportunities. The two swimming beaches on the south and east shores were renovated in 1985. In that same year, a fishhouse was built over water 11 feet deep. Measuring 24 × 40 feet and surrounded by an 8-foot walkway, the building was constructed by volunteer labor with donated funds. It is a unique feature in Iowa's state and county park system.

There are several picnic areas throughout the park and three rental shelters, each with a fireplace. An open shelter is located in the southern part. Both the north and east shelters have water and electricity. In addition, the east shelter has a kitchen and is heated for use all year round. All three shelters have playground equipment nearby.

ACTIVITIES: Swan Lake State Park offers bicycling (a trail is located along the north shore), hiking, bridle trails, snowmobiling, a baseball diamond, a nature trail, wildlife exhibits with thirty-five species of exotic and native birds and animals, camping, a concession stand, boat rental, a fishhouse, fishing, swimming, picnicking, and rental shelters.

Also present are prairie areas, an arboretum where many species of trees can be seen, and a Farmstead Museum that houses several pieces of farm machinery dating from the late 1880s up to the 1940s. Finally, educational programs are offered at the park at various times of the year.

ACKNOWLEDGMENT: Joseph Halbur, naturalist, Swan Lake State Park

FOR MORE INFORMATION:
Swan Lake State Park. Carroll: Carroll County Conservation Board.

Viking Lake State Park

LOCATION: 2 miles southeast of Stanton on Highway 34, then 2 miles south and east on Highway 115, in Montgomery County

ADDRESS: Stanton, Iowa 51573

TELEPHONE: (712) 829-2235

HISTORY: Viking Lake State Park was originally a campsite for Indians. During the construction of the dam in 1956, many Indian artifacts and

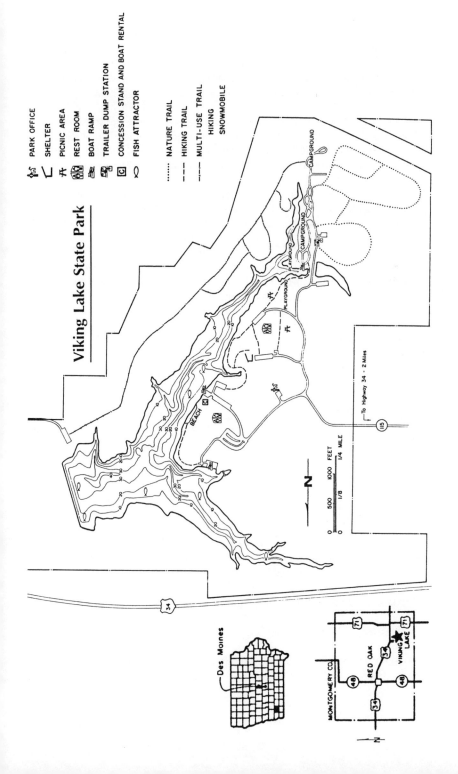

Viking Lake State Park

PARK OFFICE
SHELTER
PICNIC AREA
REST ROOM
BOAT RAMP
TRAILER DUMP STATION
CONCESSION STAND AND BOAT RENTAL
FISH ATTRACTOR

········ NATURE TRAIL
------ HIKING TRAIL
---- MULTI-USE TRAIL
HIKING
SNOWMOBILE

CAMPGROUND
CAMPGROUND
PLAYGROUND
CAMPGROUND
PLAYGROUND
BEACH

To Highway 34 - 2 Miles

N

500   1000 FEET
0   1/8   1/4 MILE

Des Moines

MONTGOMERY CO.
RED OAK
VIKING LAKE
N

burial sites were uncovered. The lake and park were developed at a cost of $415,000. The park was officially dedicated on October 13, 1957. Fifteen area communities were represented on the dedication committee. The lake was opened for fishing in 1959.

DESCRIPTION: Viking Lake covers 137 acres, has 4½ miles of shore, and a maximum depth of 46 feet. Bass, catfish, bullheads, crappies, and bluegills are present. The dam is located along the northwest shore, and hiking and snowmobile trails are located nearby. The park covers 1,000 acres, and just to the east is the West Nodaway River.

FLORA AND FAUNA: Part of the park was never developed and has abundant plant and animal life. Wildflowers are particularly common.

ACTIVITIES: The park offers hiking, fishing, picnicking, a playground, snowmobiling, supervised swimming, boat rental, a concession stand, and a boat ramp. Any size boat motors may be operated at no-wake speeds. There is also a 130-site, shaded campground with electricity at 88 sites, modern restrooms, and showers. Viking Lake is a very popular place to camp, in part due to the beauty of the campground and the nearby lake. There are two areas that provide especially nice lake views.

ACKNOWLEDGMENTS: Staff at the State Archives
Staff at Viking Lake State Park

FOR MORE INFORMATION:
Viking Lake State Park. Des Moines: Iowa Department of Natural Resources.

Walnut Woods State Park

LOCATION: A little less than ¾ of a mile east of Interstate 35 on Highway 5 in West Des Moines, then ½ mile north on 105th Street SW, then ½ mile east on 52d Avenue SW (Polk County)

ADDRESS: Box 133, R.R. 3, Des Moines, Iowa 50321

TELEPHONE: (515) 285-4502

HISTORY: Originally owned by B. F. Elbert, the park was purchased by the state on July 14, 1925, at a cost of thirty thousand dollars.

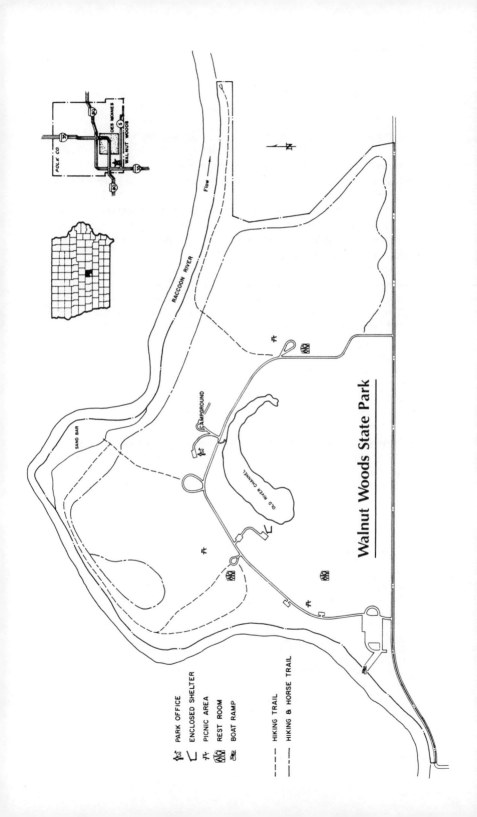

Walnut Woods State Park

PARK OFFICE
ENCLOSED SHELTER
PICNIC AREA
REST ROOM
BOAT RAMP

--- HIKING TRAIL
--- HIKING & HORSE TRAIL

RACCOON RIVER

Flow

SAND BAR

OLD RIVER CHANNEL

CAMPGROUND

POLK CO.

DES MOINES

WALNUT WOODS

N

DESCRIPTION: The 275-acre park lies in the valley of the Raccoon River. Several small ridges and shallow depressions are present, caused by past flooding.

A modern boat ramp and parking area are located near the western boundary of the park. There are several hiking and bridle trails, and in the center of the park is an 80-acre shaded picnic ground and a rental lodge. The rustic lodge was constructed during the 1930s and is a great place for group activities.

Although located just 4 miles southwest of Iowa's largest city, Des Moines, and near Interstate 35, the park's campground is rarely congested. There are 28 campsites, but they lack showers or modern restrooms. Eight of the sites do have electrical hookups.

FLORA AND FAUNA: The largest remaining strand of native black walnut trees in North America is present here. The park also has an unexpectedly high concentration of wildlife. In a three-year period, more than ninety species of birds were identified here.

ACTIVITIES: The park offers fishing, boating, camping, a beautiful rental lodge, picnicking, bird-watching, bridle trails, hiking trails, cross-country skiing, and nature study. The lodge is available during the warm weather months and is especially popular for weddings. There are no restrictions on the size of boat motors on the Raccoon River.

ACKNOWLEDGMENTS: Staff at the Iowa Department of Natural Resources
Scot Michelson, park ranger, Walnut Woods State Park

FOR MORE INFORMATION:
Walnut Woods State Park. Des Moines: Iowa Department of Natural Resources.

Waubonsie State Park

LOCATION: 4 miles south of Sidney on Highway 275, then 3 miles west on Highway 2, then 2 miles south on Highway 239, in Fremont County

ADDRESS: Hamburg, Iowa 51640

TELEPHONE: (712) 382-2786

HISTORY: On July 18, 1804, Lewis and Clark and members of their expedition began to explore this area. They found mosquitoes, rattlesnakes, and prairie grasses up to 8 feet high. However, the park staff assures visitors that all of the rattlesnakes and most of the mosquitoes have since left the park!

On the northern edge of the park is a steep hollow with an opening at the lower end. By blocking the opening with brush or fires, horses were held here, and the place became known as "Horse Thief Hollow." Legend has it that Quantrill and his gang kept stolen horses at this site until they could be sold. William Clark Quantrill (1837–65) led a band of Confederate soldiers during the Civil War. It is also said that Clyde James once lived here. Clyde was the son of Frank James.

In 1926 the state acquired the first 200 acres of the park from Ed Mincer. He also served as the park's first custodian.

In 1935 the Civilian Conservation Corps went to work in the park constructing buildings and establishing trails. The park was named in honor of Chief Waubonsie of the Pottawattamie Indians, who lived in this area in the 1840s.

DESCRIPTION: Today the park covers 1,247 acres in Iowa's beautiful loess hills. The loess hills were formed thousands of years ago by the deposition of windblown soil particles. The loess hills are found only along the Missouri River in Missouri and Iowa. Their dramatic, rugged topography and unique plants give the visitor a unique "western" experience.

A bridle trail winds around the northern area of the park and can be used by snowmobilers when there is adequate snow cover. There are more than 8 miles of bridle trails within the park. Also in the northern area are picnic grounds.

The southeastern part of the park has a total of fifty-nine campsites. A separate equestrian campground affords excellent horseback camping opportunities. Both modern (with modern restrooms and showers) and non-modern sites are offered. There are electrical outlets at twenty-two of the sites. Picnic areas and hiking trails are also present. The park has a total of 7 miles of hiking trails.

Sledding and cross-country skiing are popular winter activities on the

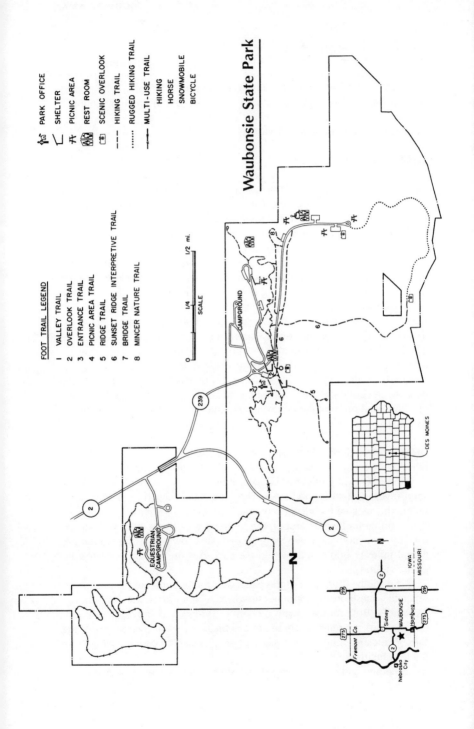

Waubonsie State Park

FOOT TRAIL LEGEND

1 VALLEY TRAIL
2 OVERLOOK TRAIL
3 ENTRANCE TRAIL
4 PICNIC AREA TRAIL
5 RIDGE TRAIL
6 SUNSET RIDGE INTERPRETIVE TRAIL
7 BRIDGE TRAIL
8 MINCER NATURE TRAIL

PARK OFFICE
SHELTER
PICNIC AREA
REST ROOM
SCENIC OVERLOOK
--- HIKING TRAIL
···· RUGGED HIKING TRAIL
—+— MULTI-USE TRAIL
      HIKING
      HORSE
      SNOWMOBILE
      BICYCLE

SCALE

0   1/4   1/2 mi.

CAMPGROUND

EQUESTRIAN CAMPGROUND

N

DES MOINES

IOWA
MISSOURI

Fremont Co.

Nebraska City
Sidney
WAUBONSIE
Hamburg

hills. Some trails remain open year round for visitors to enjoy the park's winter landscape. Present trails include Valley Nature Trail, Overlook Trail, Picnic Area Trail, Ridge Trail, Sunset Ridge Interpretive Trail, and Bridge Trail.

The Sunset Ridge Interpretive Trail begins at the shelter house in the southwestern part of the park and ends at Sunset Ridge. The trail is 1 mile long. On Sunset Ridge, visitors can view four states: Missouri, Nebraska, Kansas, and Iowa, as well as the Missouri River valley. On a clear day, distant hills up to 50 miles away are visible. Two other bluffs in the park offer similar views. One of these is Inspiration Point, located near the main parking area. Some people come here solely for the scenic views.

The wooded hills and ravines have changed little since the time of the Indians, and the autumn colors in the park are as vivid as those of north-eastern Iowa.

There are several caves in the loess hills in the park. These were probably dug by early settlers to store apples from the orchards in the vicinity. The caves also served as family dwellings during the Depression of the 1930s.

FLORA AND FAUNA: Along the nature trail and elsewhere in the park, visitors can see some of the abundant wildlife and plant life in the oak-hickory forest. There are a large variety of wildflowers and at least thirty species of trees, including a three-hundred-year-old bur oak. Some of the rare animal life that are present include Great Plains skinks, coyotes, and bald eagles.

The park also is home to some rare butterflies, including ottoe skipper, zebra swallowtail, white M-hairstreak, hoary edge, Henry's elfin, and Olympia marblewing.

ACTIVITIES: Waubonsie State Park offers bridle trails, snowmobiling, pic-nicking, camping, hiking, skiing, nature study, sledding, an interpretive trail, and scenic views.

ACKNOWLEDGMENT: Steve Eckels, park attendant, Waubonsie State Park

FOR MORE INFORMATION:

Sunset Ridge Interpretive Trail. Des Moines: Iowa Department of Natural Resources.

Tilden, F. *The State Parks: Their Meaning in American Life.* New York: Alfred A. Knopf, 1962.

Waubonsie State Park. Des Moines: Iowa Department of Natural Resources.

Wilson Island State Recreation Area

LOCATION: 5 miles west of Loveland on Highway 362 in Harrison and Pottawattamie counties

ADDRESS: R.R. 2, Missouri Valley, Iowa 51555

TELEPHONE: (712) 642-2069

HISTORY: In 1900 a shift in the channel of the Missouri River created an island here. By the 1930s, a family had settled on the island and tried to claim it. Governor George Wilson convinced the state to hang onto and preserve the island, which was later named in his honor. In the 1950s, Wilson Island was developed to provide as many recreational activities as possible without adversely affecting the wildlife and natural setting.

In 1959–60, the U.S. Army Corps of Engineers constructed a 7-mile-long channel across a bend in the Missouri River known as DeSoto Bend. A dam and road were also constructed. The purposes of the project were to create a lake that would serve as a wildlife refuge and to connect the island with the shore.

DESCRIPTION: Today Wilson Island State Recreation Area covers 577 acres along the southern border of the DeSoto Bend National Wildlife Refuge on the Missouri River floodplain. Several campgrounds were built here between 1960 and 1965 to meet the growing popularity of the refuge. A 65-site campground with modern restrooms, showers, and electricity is located in the northwestern part of the area. The other nonmodern camping areas have 67 sites. One of these campgrounds is located on the south end. The other is present in the northwestern part and has a group camping area. An interpretive trail connects the western and southern campgrounds. A rustic cabin, located in the modern campground, is available for rental on a weekly basis.

Five miles of hiking trails are present and are open to cross-country skiing and snowmobiling during the winter. Most of the trails are located in the central and southern areas of the park. A ½-mile-long trail along the Missouri River provides fishing access. Two boat ramps and a dock provide access to the river. There is no limit on horsepower for boat motors.

There are several picnic areas, one of which is along the river, and there are several picnic shelters available for reservation. An amphitheater is located to the south of the modern campground. During the summer, nature programs are offered here. The recreation area is located only 6 miles west of Interstates 29 and 680.

Bordering Wilson Island on the north is the 7,823-acre DeSoto Na-

140

tional Wildlife Refuge, managed by the U.S. Fish and Wildlife Service. The refuge has been developed for public use while at the same time providing timber, grassland, and lake habitats for wildlife. The refuge is open between 6:00 A.M. and 10:00 P.M., from mid-April until the end of September. Included in the refuge is a 750-acre oxbow lake (DeSoto Lake) that borders Wilson Island on the north. Thirty-four species of fish are known to exist in the lake. Noteworthy fish include large paddlefish, largemouth bass, channel catfish, white crappie, black crappie, walleye, perch, bluegill, and northern pike.

In the northern part of the refuge, just south of Highway 30, is a visitor center and museum. The result of four years of planning and two years of construction, and at a cost of five million dollars, the center was opened on July 11, 1981. It displays tens of thousands of artifacts from the old steamboat *Bertrand*, which sank in 1865. The collection is considered to be the best assemblage of Civil War–age artifacts found anywhere. For more information, contact: DeSoto Bend National Wildlife Refuge, R.R. 1, Box 114, Missouri Valley, Iowa 51555.

FLORA AND FAUNA: The recreation area has large areas dense with cottonwood trees and 50 acres of wildlife food plots. In October and November, and again in March and April, migrating birds reach their peak numbers here. Mid-November usually sees the greatest concentration of birds. Up to 400,000 geese and 750,000 ducks come to the refuge. Bald eagles and white pelicans are also seen.

ACTIVITIES: The campground is normally open all year long and is popular with bird-watchers in November when thousands of snow geese flock through here. Other activities offered include an interpretive trail, hiking, cross-country skiing, snowmobiling, fishing, boating, water-skiing, picnicking, nature films, and education programs. Hunting and trapping are also permitted. Game includes squirrels, rabbits, deer, quail, woodcocks, raccoons, beavers, muskrats, and coyotes. Waterfowl hunting and archery deer hunting are quite popular here.

Mushroom hunting is permitted, and in the spring, morel mushrooms can be found in abundance.

ACKNOWLEDGMENT: Bob Seitz, park ranger, Wilson Island State Recreation Area

FOR MORE INFORMATION:
U.S. Department of the Interior. *DeSoto National Wildlife Refuge.* Washington, D.C.: Government Printing Office.

Wilson Island Recreation Area. Des Moines: Iowa Department of Natural Resources.

4 Northwest Iowa

A hilltop field of prairie grasses featured at Stone State Park.

Large trees arch over winding roads at Pilot Knob State Park and Preserve.

Astride Iowa's second highest elevation, a stone tower provides a view of the surrounding countryside. (Pilot Knob)

The Carolyn Benne Nature Trail at Stone State Park.

145

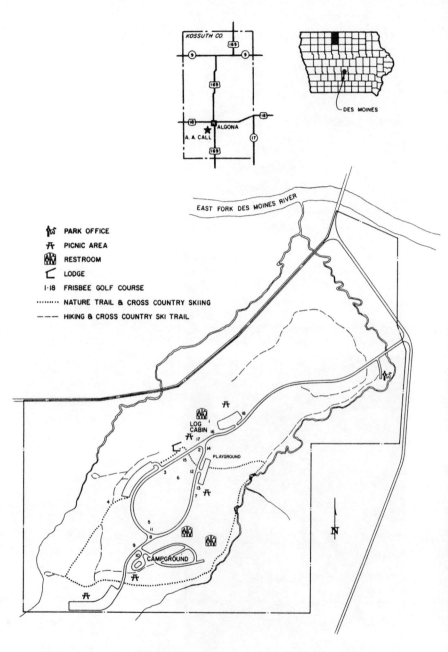

Ambrose A. Call State Park

Ambrose A. Call State Park

LOCATION: 1½ miles southwest of Algona on a county road, 1 mile west and 1 mile north of Highway 169 in Kossuth County

ADDRESS: R.R. 1, Box 264, Algona, Iowa 50511

TELEPHONE: (515) 295-3669

HISTORY: The brothers Ambrose and Asa Call were the first settlers here in 1854. While their original log cabin no longer exists, another log cabin was moved to the site from nearby property years ago. The park was dedicated in 1929. The first caretaker, Paul Wille, developed trails throughout the park. The Civilian Conservation Corps assisted in the work in 1933. During World War II German POWs from the prisoner-of-war camp in Algona worked in the park. The state, local citizens, and organizations also worked to develop the park in its early days.

DESCRIPTION: Ambrose A. Call State Park covers 130 acres along a tributary of the east fork of the Des Moines River. The river runs along the northeast corner of the park and is noted for catfish and northern pike fishing. The hills in the park were the work of glaciers of the Wisconsin Glacial Stage from fifteen thousand to twenty thousand years ago.

FLORA: The park contains one of the largest tracts of timber, mainly black walnuts and oaks, in heavily farmed Kossuth County. There are also abundant spring wildflowers.

ACTIVITIES: A. A. Call offers 32 campsites, all lacking showers, modern restrooms, and electricity. There is an eighteen-hole Frisbee golf course in the center of the park. Also available are a scenic rental lodge, nature study, fishing, picnicking, and 5 miles of hiking trails. The area has become quite popular for cross-country skiing in the winter. Recent additions to the park include a self-guided nature trail (1½ miles) and a bulletin board offering information on nature. Various trees are identified by signs along the trail. The bulletin board has descriptions, photos, and specimens of local plant life. Camping in May, when the wildflowers are in bloom, or in October, after the first frost, offers great scenic views.

ACKNOWLEDGMENT: Ron Jones, park ranger, Ambrose A. Call State Park

FOR MORE INFORMATION:
   Ambrose A. Call State Park. Des Moines: Iowa Department of Natural Resources.

Bigelow State Park

LOCATION: 2 miles west of Salix on paved County Road K-25 in Woodbury County

ADDRESS: Woodbury County Conservation Board, Sioux City, Iowa 51101

TELEPHONE: (712) 279-6488 (Woodbury County Conservation Board)

HISTORY: The land was donated to the state by the Bigelow family. In 1971 the Woodbury County Conservation Board was granted a maintenance agreement from the state for the park. Since then, substantial improvements have been made by the county. Several new facilities were built, and the park was totally renovated. In 1975 12 acres were added to the park's 24. In 1978 the Dale G. Bell Memorial Arboretum was dedicated. He was a member of the Woodbury County Conservation Board. In 1982 new boat and fishing docks were completed.

DESCRIPTION: Bigelow State Park is located just west of the Salix interchange on Interstate 29, about 15 miles south of Sioux City. The park comprises 36 acres of timber along the south shore of Brown's Lake, a 200-acre oxbow lake. The lake, and several like it, was formed around the turn of the century by shifts in the course of the meandering Missouri River. There is also a 1,000-acre wildlife area in the vicinity, offering lake-marsh, timber, and upland habitats. The park has a full-time ranger.

ACTIVITIES: The park has a campground with electricity, modern restrooms, and showers. An enclosed shelter is available for rental, and a small open shelter is available on a first-come basis. The park offers hiking, picnicking, a boat ramp, boat rental (no limit on horsepower for boat motors), swimming, and snowmobiling. There is a concession stand near the beach. The natural beach has been a favorite area for visitors, and the park is popular with bird-watchers. Largemouth bass, northern pike, channel catfish, and others can be caught in the lake. Waterfowl, rabbit, and pheasant hunting are allowed in the wildlife refuge.

ACKNOWLEDGMENT: Rick Schneider, Woodbury County Conservation Board, Sioux City

FOR MORE INFORMATION:
History of Woodbury County, Iowa. Sioux City: Woodbury County Genealogical Society, 1984.
Outdoor Recreation in Woodbury County. Sioux City: Woodbury

County Conservation Board.
Woodbury County Parks and Recreation Areas. Sioux City: Woodbury County Conservation Board.

Black Hawk Lake State Park

LOCATION: Southeastern edge of Lake View on Highway 243 in Sac County

ADDRESS: P.O. Box 7, Lake View, Iowa 51450

TELEPHONE: (712) 657-2639

HISTORY: In the early 1800s, the French knew this lake as "Boyer Lake." In 1935 Black Hawk Lake was dedicated as a state park. It was named in honor of Chief Black Hawk of the Sac and Fox Indians. Between 1936 and 1938, the Civilian Conservation Corps did much work in the park, including constructing two shelters, a fish hatchery, and a round shelter house (the "Witch's Tower").

The park has been a popular recreation area for many years. However, a severe winterkill in 1974–75, a drought in 1976, and another winterkill in 1977 left the lake devoid of game fish. The carp and buffalo fish, being hardier, survived. In 1978 aerators were installed in the lake to help prevent winterkills, and the rough fish were killed off by chemicals. In 1979 and 1980, massive restocking of walleye, tiger muskie, channel catfish, crappie, perch, sunfish, bluegill, and largemouth bass was carried out.

DESCRIPTION: The lake, formed during the Wisconsin glacial stage, covers 925 acres. The park comprises 86 acres. Some of the best fishing can be done in the northwestern part of the lake where the water reaches its maximum depth of 12 feet. There is no restriction on size of boat motors. A marina is located on the northeast shore.

The park's 176-site campground is located near the southeastern part of the lake and features playground equipment, modern restrooms, showers, and 68 sites with electricity. The campground is frequently filled to capacity.

Just west of Black Hawk Lake is the smaller Arrowhead Lake. This lake has a boat dock on the northwest shore and picnic areas. It offers sunfish, bass, and bullhead fishing.

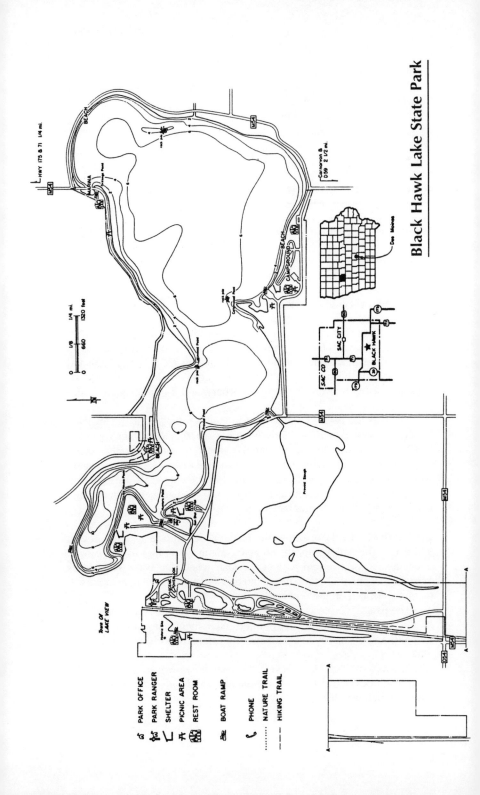

Black Hawk Lake State Park

PARK OFFICE
PARK RANGER
SHELTER
PICNIC AREA
REST ROOM
BOAT RAMP
PHONE
NATURE TRAIL
HIKING TRAIL

Between the southern parts of the two lakes is Provost Slough. This area and Arrowhead Lake are designated a wildlife refuge in the spring and fall.

South of Black Hawk Lake is Black Hawk Marsh, a 206-acre marsh and grass habitat where waterfowl and pheasant may be hunted. Black Hawk Lake itself is also open to waterfowl hunting.

FLORA AND FAUNA: Black Hawk Lake State Park is home to abundant trees and plants, including at least sixteen species of wildflowers. Black Hawk Lake, Arrowhead Lake, and Provost Slough are all popular for native birds and migrating shorebirds and gulls. In the spring and fall, bird-watchers come to see Canadian geese, mallards, redheads, blue-winged teal, green-winged teal, pelicans, and warblers. In summer, herons, bitterns, and other marsh birds are present. Chickadees, nuthatches, cardinals, blue jays, and several species of sparrows may be seen in the winter.

ACTIVITIES: Today Black Hawk Lake State Park is one of the most popular state parks in Iowa, attracting not only Iowans but a large number of out-of-state visitors as well. The lake, the picnic areas with shelters (available for reservation), the campground, the good paved road system, and the nearby restaurants seem to be the main reasons for the park's popularity. In the winter, snowmobiling, ice-skating, and iceboating are enjoyed by many. Iceboats have reached speeds up to one hundred miles an hour on the frozen lake.

The park also offers boating, boat rental, unsupervised swimming, nature programs, playground equipment, hiking, nature trails, and bird-watching. Waterfowl hunting is permitted on the lake and in the nearby game management area. The lake offers catfish, crappies, and other fish for fishermen.

A 1.6-mile-long nature trail was dedicated to Bernard "Stubb" Severson for his dedication to conservation. Along the trail, visitors can view the Witch's Tower (the unusual-looking shelter house) and a large variety of plants and trees.

ACKNOWLEDGMENT: Eric Haakenson, park attendant, Black Hawk Lake State Park

FOR MORE INFORMATION:

Bernard "Stubb" Severson Trail. Des Moines: Iowa Department of Natural Resources.

Black Hawk Lake State Park. Des Moines: Iowa Department of Natural Resources.

Cole, C. *I Am a Man: The Indian Black Hawk.* Iowa City: State Historical Society of Iowa, 1983.

Brushy Creek State Recreation Area

LOCATION: 4 miles east of Lehigh on County Road D-46 in Webster County

ADDRESS: R.R. 1, Box 150, Lehigh, Iowa 50557

TELEPHONE: (515) 359-2501

HISTORY: Plans to acquire and develop 4,200 acres in Webster County were approved by the Iowa Conservation Commission in the 1960s. Such an area was needed because of the lack of a major body of recreational water in the area. An estimated 800,000 people live within 90 miles of the site.

Acquisition of the land began in 1968 and was completed in 1975 at a cost of $2.6 million. Plans for a lake and outdoor recreation facility development have been delayed, but some trail and campground development work has been carried out. It is anticipated that a 690-acre lake will be completed in the early 1990s and that extensive outdoor recreational development will take place. Additional land has been purchased south of the area, extending to the Des Moines River. When all land acquisition is completed, Brushy Creek will exceed 6,000 acres in size.

DESCRIPTION: Brushy Creek is Iowa's second largest state-owned recreation area with 4,205 acres (Volga River is larger). It is comprised of upland and timber habitats, with patches of native prairie. The terrain is hilly, with steep slopes along the creek and large glacial boulders. To the west of the creek, near the south end of the park, Indian mounds are present. A several-hundred-acre area in this location has been dedicated as a state preserve because of its archaeological, natural, and geological resources. Evidence of bison kills has been discovered here as far back as the Archaic Culture, up to five thousand years ago.

The recreation area has emerged as one of the top equestrian sites in Iowa. At times, as many as several hundred riders from throughout Iowa and neighboring states utilize Brushy Creek. Nearly 30 miles of bridle trails and 16 miles of snowmobile trails are offered. The area is also popular with cross-country skiers.

Brushy Creek features a large equestrian campground, with 125 sites (including 10 with electricity). No modern restroom or shower buildings are available yet at Brushy Creek, although water is available in the campground. A pleasant picnic area is located along Brushy Creek in the southern portion of the park.

FLORA AND FAUNA: Many species of wildlife are present, including the very rare woodland vole, especially in the Brushy Creek State Preserve located in the southwestern portion of the area. Also present is a wide variety of wildflowers.

ACTIVITIES: Brushy Creek is a tributary of the Des Moines River and offers fishing. Hunting is allowed throughout the area, except in the campground. Deer, squirrel, pheasant, turkey, gray partridge, quail, and rabbit can be hunted. The recreation area also offers bridle trails, hiking, nature study, snowmobiling, cross-country skiing, mushroom hunting, camping, picnicking, and bird-watching.

ACKNOWLEDGMENTS: Bill Bird, park ranger, and Denny Ewers, park attendant, Brushy Creek State Recreation Area

FOR MORE INFORMATION:
Brushy Creek Recreation Area. Des Moines: Iowa Department of Natural Resources.

Cayler Prairie State Preserve

LOCATION: 3 miles east and 2 miles south of Lake Park on a county road in Dickinson County

HISTORY: Cayler Prairie was purchased by the state in 1960. In 1966 the National Park Service designated it as a national landmark, and on May 5, 1971, it was dedicated as a state preserve.

DESCRIPTION: The 160-acre native prairie is one of Iowa's largest. It has never been plowed and gives visitors an idea of how the state must have looked to the early pioneers. Seventy-five acres of the preserve are rolling prairie, and the rest is lowland prairie with areas that are intermediate (between upland and lowland). The Little Sioux River runs along the eastern part of the preserve. Eskers can be seen along the river. These are ridges of sand and gravel deposited by water passing through tunnels beneath the surface of a glacier. The glacier had stopped advancing and was melting. Eskers are not commonly found in Iowa. These are from the Wisconsin Glacial Stage and are about thirteen thousand years old.

There is a parking area on the west side of the preserve along a gravel road.

FLORA AND FAUNA: Cayler Prairie is home to more than 260 species of plants, including many endangered or rare species. At least 20 species of birds inhabit or frequently visit the preserve. The prairie is also home to several mammals, reptiles, and amphibians. Insects are numerous, including several kinds of butterflies. Some mounds of harvester ants are decades old and are nearly 1 foot high and 1 yard in diameter.

Extensive studies of the flora and fauna in the prairie have been, and are still being, conducted by the Iowa Lakeside Laboratory at Wahpeton.

ACTIVITIES: Pheasants and rabbits may be hunted. Other activities are restricted to those that will not harm the preserve, such as nature study and bird-watching.

ACKNOWLEDGMENT: Iowa Great Lakes Chamber of Commerce, Spirit Lake

FOR MORE INFORMATION:
Visitor's Guide to Cayler Prairie. Des Moines: Iowa Department of Natural Resources.

Dolliver Memorial State Park

LOCATION: The south entrance is located 1½ miles west of Lehigh on Highway 50, then 1 mile north; the north entrance is located 2 miles south of Coalville on County Road P-59, then 3 miles east and southeast on another county road (Webster County).

ADDRESS: Lehigh, Iowa 50557

TELEPHONE: (515) 359-2539

HISTORY: The area was a popular site with Indians. Here they built mounds on top of one of the highest spots in Iowa. Some accounts claim that they used a hollow in this area to trap and slaughter buffalo, elk, and deer (Boneyard Hollow). The site may have been used as early as the Woodland Culture. A rocky area across the Des Moines River at the south end of the park (Franke's Riffle) is supposedly the remains of a small dam that Indians used to entrap fish. The Indians also came to the bluffs on scenic Prairie Creek to use the deposit of the mineral copperas (unique because of its abundance) for dyes and paint.

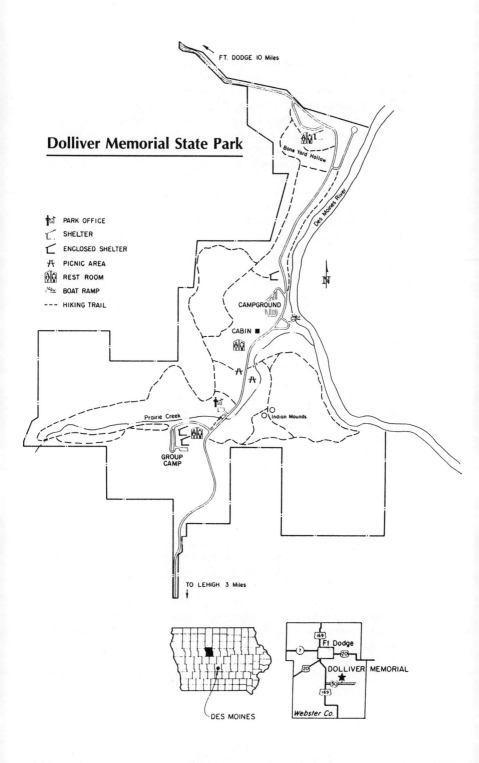

Dolliver Memorial State Park

FT. DODGE 10 Miles

Bone Yard Hollow

Des Moines River

PARK OFFICE
SHELTER
ENCLOSED SHELTER
PICNIC AREA
REST ROOM
BOAT RAMP
HIKING TRAIL

N

CAMPGROUND

CABIN ■

Prairie Creek

Indian Mounds

GROUP CAMP

TO LEHIGH 3 Miles

DES MOINES

169
7
Ft Dodge
20
20
DOLLIVER MEMORIAL
50
169
Webster Co.

In 1912 a picnicker uncovered a lead plaque in Boneyard Hollow that was inscribed in Latin. The inscription indicated that it had been placed there by the French missionary Father Hennepin in 1701. The plaque was quickly declared a hoax, and two men then confessed to the prank. However, two of the experts that examined the site were Edgar Harlan of the state archives and Dr. L. H. Pammel, who was head of the botany department at Iowa State College (now Iowa State University). They saw how beautiful the area was and were instrumental in including it in the state park system.

The park was dedicated on June 28, 1925, with approximately fourteen thousand people attending. The original 400 acres were purchased at a total cost of $48,500. Dolliver became the third state park in Iowa, after Backbone and Lacey-Keosauqua. In the center of the park, on a sandstone outcrop above a spring, a bronze memorial plaque was placed. It bears the likeness of Jonathan P. Dolliver and was designed by Lorado Taft (1860–1936), one of America's leading sculptors. Dolliver moved to Iowa at the age of twenty-one and lived in this area. He was a U.S. senator from 1900 until his death in 1910.

DESCRIPTION: The 572-acre Dolliver Memorial State Park has hills and deep ravines with dramatic slopes. Boneyard Hollow, in the northern part of the park, has high sandstone bluffs covered with Virginia creeper. Only two other state parks in Iowa have sandstone bluffs of this size. The bluffs were laid down during the Pennsylvanian Period and are part of the Floris Formation. In this area, the bluffs exhibit extreme examples of cross-bedding in which thin layers were deposited at sharp angles to the normal horizontal bedding plane. The campground is located to the south of the hollow.

The Indian mounds area is located in the east central part of the park, near Prairie Creek and the Des Moines River. Hiking in this area is rigorous at times, but from the tops of the hills, visitors have scenic views of the park and river.

Butternut Grove is located south of Prairie Creek, in the south central area of the park. It is a popular picnic area with large butternut trees. The group camp is located here. It is available for rent and includes sleeping cabins, a dining hall, and a modern restroom and shower building. The Copperas Beds Trail begins at the picnic grounds.

The copperas beds are located west of Butternut Grove, in the western part of the park. They can be reached by foot only. Located here is the only suspended footbridge in an Iowa state park. It spans Prairie Creek. The large sandstone bluff here is up to 150 feet high. The upper parts of the bluff contain an abundance of copperas, sulphur, and iron. During heavy rains, the minerals leach down the bluff and into Prairie Creek. Indians used the colorful deposits, the stories say, for paint and dye.

Other areas of the park include:

- Steamboat Rock, located at the north end of the park. This was a popular area for boats to land and pick up supplies while traveling on the Des Moines River.
- Todd's Island, located near the south end of the park. In the 1860s, a sawmill was built here.

FLORA AND FAUNA: Nearly every species of plant native to central Iowa can be found in the prairie remnants, forest, and transition areas of Dolliver Park. The southern part of the park is the first to bloom in the spring and the first to change color in autumn. There is also an abundance of wildlife.

ACTIVITIES: Dolliver Memorial Park has 22 campsites with electricity and 20 without, and modern restrooms and showers. There are two open shelters that may be reserved, two scenic lodges available for reservations, and the group camp with ten cabins, a mess hall, and a lodge. A stone rental cabin is located near the campground and offers family sleeping and cooking facilities. The shower and restroom building is located nearby.

The park offers 6 miles of trails for hiking, cross-country skiing, several picnic areas, bird-watching, a boat ramp on the Des Moines River, scenic views, and playground equipment. In the Des Moines River, fishermen may catch catfish, smallmouth bass, walleyes, and even an occasional northern pike. Prairie Creek also offers smallmouth bass fishing. Children enjoy wading in beautiful Prairie Creek. Canoeing on the river from Kalo to the park (about 5 miles) has become a popular activity.

ACKNOWLEDGMENT: Steve Bell, park ranger, Dolliver Memorial State Park

FOR MORE INFORMATION:
Dolliver State Park. Des Moines: Iowa Department of Natural Resources.

Eagle Lake State Park

LOCATION: 3 miles east and 1 mile north of Britt off Highway 18 in Hancock County

ADDRESS: Hancock County Conservation Board, Garner, Iowa 50438

TELEPHONE: (515) 932-2720 (Hancock County Conservation Board)

HISTORY: Eagle Lake is actually a marsh that has been popular with hunters since the turn of the century. In 1916 the maximum depth of the lake was less than 5 feet. A dam and water-control system on the north shore maintained the water level to assure that the lake would remain a marsh and continue to attract waterfowl.

In 1924 citizens of Britt purchased 13 acres along Eagle Lake. A landowner donated an additional 9 acres, which was then deeded to the state to develop a park. In 1935 the state built a shelter here.

In 1974 the Iowa Conservation Commission decided to take action against rising water levels that were threatening the marsh habitat. While hunters were in favor of the action, some local citizens voiced opposition. However, by May of that year, the water level had been substantially reduced, and new vegetation was allowed to grow.

DESCRIPTION: The lake covers 900 acres, and the park covers 21 acres. Forty-six acres along the west shore of the marsh have been designated a forest preserve.

FLORA AND FAUNA: Eagle Lake is an excellent shallow lake and marsh habitat for waterfowl. There is also a large muskrat population. The marsh has smartweed, pitchforks, roundstem bulrush, cattail, river bulrush, and wild rice.

ACTIVITIES: The park offers picnicking, nature study, camping (no electricity), and hiking. Waterfowl and pheasant hunting are permitted nearby.

ACKNOWLEDGMENT: Staff at Iowa Department of Natural Resources

Ellsworth Park

LOCATION: 8 miles west of Forest City on County Road B-14 in Hancock County

ADDRESS: Hancock County Conservation Board, Garner, Iowa 50438

TELEPHONE: (515) 923-2720 (Hancock County Conservation Board)

DESCRIPTION: The 130-acre park is situated on the east shore of Crystal Lake, a natural lake that covers 261 acres. The park is home to the "World's Largest Bullhead." At 17 feet, 8 inches in length, and weighing 1,650 pounds, the fish is actually a sculpture designed by Carl Frick.
The park is open from 7:00 A.M. until 10:00 P.M. daily.

ACTIVITIES: The park offers camping with electricity, picnicking, swimming, and fishing. Waterfowl and pheasant hunting are allowed nearby. A boat ramp is available, and there is no restriction on the size of boat motors. There are shelters available to the public on a first-come basis, and playground equipment.

ACKNOWLEDGMENT: Richard Carney, mayor, Crystal Lake

Emerson Bay Recreation Area

LOCATION: 2½ miles north of Milford on Highway 86 in Dickinson County

ADDRESS: Gull Point State Park, R.R. 2, Milford, Iowa 51351

TELEPHONE: (712) 337-3211 (Gull Point State Park)

DESCRIPTION: Located on the southwest shore of West Okoboji Lake, Emerson Bay Recreation Area comprises 120 acres and has a 117-site campground with showers and modern restrooms. Sixty of the sites have electrical hookups. During the summer, the conveniently located boat ramp and parking area are heavily used because of their location along the west shore of the 3,800-acre lake, which is sheltered from most summer winds. There is no limit on horsepower for boat motors. The area is located only 1 mile south of Gull Point State Park.

Other state-owned parks and preserves in the area include Gardner-Sharp Cabin, Gull Point State Park, Isthmus Access, Lower Gar Access, Marble Beach Recreation Area, Mini-Wakan State Park, Pikes Point State Park, Pillsbury Point, Trappers Bay, and Triboji Beach.

ACTIVITIES: The area offers camping, picnicking, unsupervised swimming, fishing, and snowmobiling. There is a boat ramp within the area, and boat rental is available nearby. The adjacent "light house point" area offers picnicking, an open shelter, and a lake observation tower.

FOR MORE INFORMATION:
Iowa Great Lakes Region. Des Moines: Iowa Department of Natural Resources.

Fort Defiance State Park

LOCATION: 1 mile west of Estherville in Emmet County

ADDRESS: Estherville, Iowa 51334

TELEPHONE: (712) 362-2078

HISTORY: During the Sioux War of 1862, which took place in southern Minnesota, settlers in Iowa feared that the fighting would spread. Because federal soldiers were engaged in the Civil War, the government was unable to provide protection. The citizens of Estherville built a wooden stockade around the schoolhouse located one block west and two blocks south of the town square. The building served as a hospital and living quarters.

The fort became active on September 24, 1862, and was one of a string of five forts built to protect northwest Iowa from Indian attacks. The state of Iowa raised five companies of volunteers to man the forts. These were called the Northern Iowa Border Brigade. Company A was located at Fort Defiance under the command of Captain William Ingham from Kossuth County.

The fort was occupied for about a year until the fall of 1863. There had been no major Indian attacks, and tensions eased. In 1866, three years after the troops left, the stockade was torn down and the lumber was used to

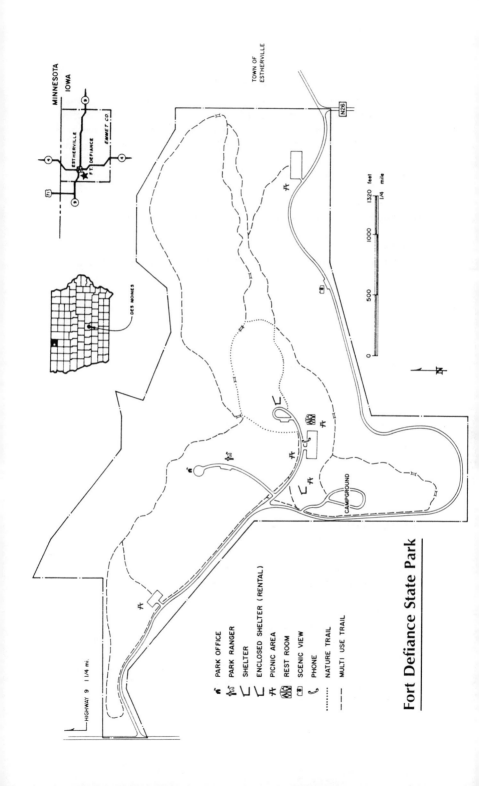

Fort Defiance State Park

build cabins. Nothing of the fort remains today. However, in 1911, a 25-foot-high Fort Defiance monument was erected by the Okamanpadu chapter of the Daughters of the American Revolution (DAR). It is located near the northwest corner of the courthouse.

In the 1920s, the DAR and other local citizens purchased 50 acres for the development of a state park, and the state agreed to match their effort. Early development of the park carried out by the state included roads and a unique, fortlike cedar-log lodge with fireplace. Dedication of the park was held on October 15, 1931.

DESCRIPTION: Today the 181-acre park includes a hill that overlooks the original site of the fort. It is located 12 miles east of the Iowa great lakes area.

The central area of the park has hiking trails, an interpretive trail, and a unique rental lodge. Bridle trails are found in both the central and northern areas. The campground is located in the southwestern portion of the park. In the southeastern part of the park is a scenic-view area. Paved roads provide vehicle access within the park, and snowmobiling is permitted on portions of these roads.

FLORA: The park is heavily wooded and has many species of trees, especially oaks and locusts. Wildflowers and prairie grasses can also be found. The endangered prairie bush clover occurs here.

ACTIVITIES: Fort Defiance State Park offers a popular 32-site campground with electricity (lacking modern restrooms or showers), an interpretive trail, hiking trails, bridle trails, scenic views, picnicking, fishing in the west fork of the Des Moines River, snowmobiling, and a lodge that is available to the public on a rental basis. Sledding and cross-country skiing have become popular here.

FOR MORE INFORMATION:
Fort Defiance State Park. Des Moines: Iowa Department of Natural Resources.

Frank A. Gotch State Park

LOCATION: 2 miles south of Humboldt, and 2 miles east of Highway 169, on a county road in Humboldt County

ADDRESS: Humboldt County Conservation Board, Humboldt, Iowa 50548

TELEPHONE: (515) 332-4087 (Humboldt County Conservation Board)

HISTORY: In 1825 Frenchmen established a small fort here, Fort Confederation. This was one of the first three French posts established in Iowa. When other settlers arrived twenty to thirty years later, they could find very little evidence of the fort, and nothing remains of it today. The fort was reportedly built near the junction of the east and west forks of the Des Moines River.

The state acquired the land in 1942. It had been used as a state park for several years before it was officially dedicated Frank A. Gotch State Park in April 1949. Gotch (1877–1917), a native of Humboldt, was the Wrestling Champion of the World from 1908 until his retirement in 1913. Major developments in the park were undertaken in the 1960s by the Humboldt and Dakota City junior chamber of commerce. In cooperation with the Humboldt County Board of Supervisors, they placed a memorial plaque in the park honoring Gotch. Other local citizens, organizations, and businesses assisted in constructing a six-thousand-dollar shelter house, which is open to the public on a first-come basis.

DESCRIPTION: The park covers 67 acres along the east and west forks of the Des Moines River. There are three picnic shelters, one of which has a fireplace and overlooks the junction of the two rivers.

ACTIVITIES: The park has a popular campground with electricity, modern restrooms, and showers, and offers picnicking, a large playground, and fishing in both rivers.

FOR MORE INFORMATION:
De Grote, O. H. *History of the City of Humboldt.* Humboldt: Jaqua Printing Company, 1963.

Gardner-Sharp Cabin Historical Site

LOCATION: In Arnolds Park off Highway 71 in Dickinson County

TELEPHONE: (712) 332-7248 (during open season)

HISTORY: Rowland Gardner settled here on July 16, 1856, with his family. On March 8, 1857, a band of renegade Sioux Indians attacked the cabin. They then began a series of attacks on nearby cabins that became known as the "Spirit Lake Massacre." By the end of the attacks on March 13, forty settlers had been killed and four women taken hostage.

In May of 1857, other Indians made two deals with the band of Sioux in exchange for two of the women hostages. The other two had been killed. One of the freed hostages was Abigail Gardner, the daughter of Rowland.

In 1891 Abigail purchased her father's old cabin. She died in 1921, but her family continued to own the cabin until her grandson Albert gave it to the state. The local Federated Women's Clubs maintained the property until 1959 when the State Historical Society was given the job.

In the 1960s, a visitor center with museum displays was constructed and is open from Memorial Day to Labor Day. The cabin was furnished with pioneer items and was restored in 1975 to its original 1856 appearance. On August 4, 1975, the cabin was officially dedicated as a state historical site.

DESCRIPTION: The cabin and visitor center are located at what is now Pillsbury Point. Also at Pillsbury Point are a mass grave of some of the victims, the family burial plot of the Gardners, plaques marking the sites of the Gardner and Luce cabins, and the Spirit Lake Massacre Monument. On July 25, 1895, the monument was dedicated. It bears the names of the victims on bronze tablets.

Other state facilities in the area include Emerson Bay, Gull Point State Park, Isthmus Access, Lower Gar Access, Marble Beach, Mini-Wakan State Park, Pikes Point State Park, Pillsbury Point, Trappers Bay, and Triboji Beach.

ACKNOWLEDGMENT: Iowa Great Lakes Area Chamber of Commerce, Spirit Lake

FOR MORE INFORMATION:
The Gardner Cabin. Des Moines: Iowa State Historical Society.
Gardner-Sharp, A. History of the Spirit Lake Massacre. Abbie Gardner-Sharp, 1885.

Lee, L. P. *History of the Spirit Lake Massacre.* Iowa City: State Historical Society of Iowa, 1971.

The Spirit Lake Massacre. Spirit Lake: National Society Daughters of
the American Revolution, Ladies of the Lake Chapter.

Gull Point State Park

LOCATION: 3½ miles north of Milford on Highway 86 in Dickinson
County

ADDRESS: R.R. 2, Milford, Iowa 51351

TELEPHONE: (712) 337-3211

HISTORY: The park was acquired through separate purchases by the state.
In the early 1930s, four thousand dollars was paid to D. W. and Lena S.
Dickinson for some of the property. The sum of nine hundred dollars was
also spent to acquire property belonging to the Pritchard estate. A small
portion of land was donated to the state on June 18, 1934, courtesy of the
West Okoboji Golf and Country Club. These acquisitions comprised the
early park, which was officially named on March 8, 1935.

The park was developed in the 1930s. In 1934 a large and beautiful
shelter was constructed out of glacial boulders found in the area. Funding
to purchase and develop the park was provided by the state and the Citizens of Okoboji Lake District, which donated five thousand dollars in
1933. Construction in the park was done by the Civilian Conservation
Corps.

Another portion of the park was a golf course from 1917 until the start
of World War II. In 1946 the course was opened again but was abandoned
after a year and became pasture. Two years later, the Prairie Gold Boy Scout
Council bought the land and established a scout camp. In 1974 they sold it
to the state, and it became a part of Gull Point State Park.

DESCRIPTION: This 165-acre park is a peninsula surrounded on three sides
by West Okoboji Lake and with a canal on the fourth side. It is located
along the west shore of the lake and is a popular gathering place for gulls.

West Okoboji Lake is the second largest glacial lake in Iowa. It was
formed about fourteen thousand years ago by a retreating glacier during the

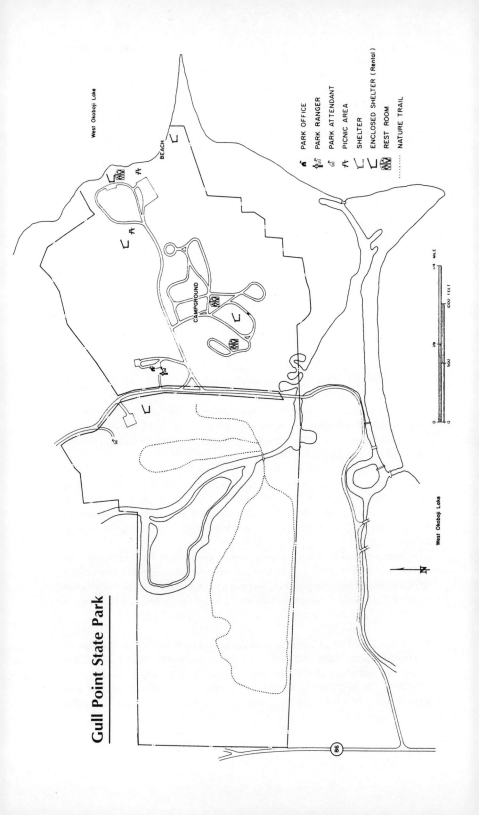

Gull Point State Park

West Okoboji Lake

West Okoboji Lake

BEACH

CAMPGROUND

PARK OFFICE
PARK RANGER
PARK ATTENDANT
PICNIC AREA
SHELTER
ENCLOSED SHELTER (Rental)
REST ROOM
NATURE TRAIL

1/4 MILE

0   1/8   500   1000 FEET

N

86

Wisconsin Glacial Stage. Covering 3,847 acres and with a maximum depth of 150 feet, the lake is fed by constantly flowing underground springs and is noted for its crystal clear water.

A water patrol station is located nearby. Other state-owned parks and preserves in the area include Emerson Bay, Gardner-Sharp Cabin, Isthmus Access, Lower Gar Access, Marble Beach, Mini-Wakan State Park, Pikes Point State Park, Pillsbury Point, Trappers Bay, and Triboji Beach.

ACTIVITIES: The park has a 112-unit campground with electricity (at 62 sites), modern restrooms, and showers. A large and beautiful stone lodge is available for rental. A playground is also present. Other facilities provide for picnicking with open shelters available for rental, hiking, unsupervised swimming, snowmobiling, and cross-country skiing. There is a 1.3-mile self-guided nature trail located opposite the main entrance to the park. Forty-five minutes is required to complete the trail. Boating and fishing are popular activities on the lake, with over 100,000 boaters and fishermen annually. Fish species common in the lake include walleyes, northern pike, smallmouth bass, white bass, perch, bluegills, crappies, catfish, and bullheads. The lake is also popular with waterfowl hunters.

ACKNOWLEDGMENTS: Staff at the State Archives
Staff at Gull Point State Park

FOR MORE INFORMATION:
Iowa Great Lakes Region. Des Moines: Iowa Department of Natural Resources.

Heery Woods State Park

LOCATION: Southern edge of Clarksville off Highway 188 in Butler County

ADDRESS: Clarksville, Iowa 50619

TELEPHONE: (319) 278-4237

HISTORY: Heery Woods State Park was named after John Heery, the first settler in Butler County. In 1852 Mr. Heery moved here from Milton, Wisconsin. The land remained in the Heery family until 1935, when 385 acres

167

were sold to the state by John Heery's granddaughters at a cost of $5,786.70 ($15 an acre). The park was developed in the 1930s by the Works Progress Administration and others. Today the park is managed by the Butler County Conservation Board.

DESCRIPTION: The park comprises 380 acres along both banks of the Shell Rock River. An enclosed lodge, built from stone quarried nearby, has modern restrooms and is located on a hill overlooking the river to the north. Available to the public on a rental basis, the lodge is frequently booked up to a year in advance. In 1983 another shelter was moved to the north side of the park and is available to the public on a first-come basis. A park ranger residence and the headquarters of the Butler County Conservation Board are located within the park.

FLORA AND FAUNA: The park is heavily wooded. Hickory and oak trees are the most prevalent, but other trees and shrubs are present and wildflowers are abundant. Wildlife is common in the park, including deer and a wide variety of birds.

ACTIVITIES: The park offers a campground with electricity, picnicking, hiking, bird-watching, rental lodge, nature study, mushroom hunting, scenic views, and fishing and boating in the Shell Rock River.

ACKNOWLEDGMENTS: Librarian, Allison Public Library
Staff at the Butler County Conservation Board, Clarksville

Isthmus Access

LOCATION: North shore of East Okoboji Lake off Highway 9, just east of the town of Spirit Lake, in Dickinson County

ADDRESS: Gull Point State Park, R.R. 2, Milford, Iowa 51351

TELEPHONE: (712) 337-3211 (Gull Point State Park)

DESCRIPTION: Covering 7 acres, Isthmus Access lies between East Okoboji and Spirit lakes. East Okoboji Lake covers 1,835 acres.

To the east of the area is the Spirit Lake fish hatchery. The present facility, built in 1963 and expanded in 1978, has twenty rearing ponds and a visitors center with five large aquariums of native fish on display. Twelve million walleyes are hatched here each year. Other fish produced include muskellunge, northern pike, and tiger muskie. The best time to visit the hatchery is in April or May when hatchery activity has begun. During this time, the hatchery remains open twenty-four hours a day. For the rest of the year, the hatchery is open on weekdays, and also on weekends and holidays during the summer. The staff can answer most questions about fish and fishing in Iowa's great lakes region, and brochures are available.

Other state-owned facilities in the area include Emerson Bay, Gardner-Sharp Cabin, Gull Point State Park, Lower Gar Access, Marble Beach, Mini-Wakan State Park, Pikes Point State Park, Pillsbury Point, Trappers Bay, and Triboji Beach.

ACTIVITIES: The Isthmus Access area is very popular for picnicking and fishing. Other activities include snowmobiling and unsupervised swimming. A boat ramp is located nearby. East Okoboji Lake offers bullhead, walleye, and perch fishing, among others.

FOR MORE INFORMATION:
Iowa Great Lakes Region. Des Moines: Iowa Department of Natural Resources.

Kalsow Prairie State Preserve

LOCATION: 4½ miles north of Manson on County Road N-65, then around 1 mile west, in Pocahontas County

HISTORY: The land was purchased in 1949 by the state and was dedicated a state preserve in 1968.

DESCRIPTION: Kalsow Prairie State Preserve is primarily composed of upland prairie with areas of lowland prairie. It covers 160 acres.

FLORA AND FAUNA: At least 240 species of plants have been identified here. Perhaps the prairie's biggest attraction is the abundance and variety of wildflowers; at least thirty species can be found. Also present are eight species of reptiles and amphibians, twenty species of mammals, and many species of birds.

ACTIVITIES: The prairie offers nature study. It is open for public hunting.

169

Lake Cornelia Park

LOCATION: Just east of Clarion on Highway 3, then around 4 miles north on paved County Road R-45, in Wright County

ADDRESS: Clarion, Iowa 50525

TELEPHONE: (515) 532-3185

HISTORY: On September 25, 1920, the Clarion Commercial Club presented the State Board of Conservation with a petition requesting that a 600-foot strip of land between Little Wall Lake and Mud Lake be condemned and then acquired by the state. Citizens were hoping to prevent the planned digging of a well to drain the lakes. Little Wall Lake was later renamed Lake Cornelia, and the land was the start of Lake Cornelia Park. In the 1940s, the lake was dredged to deepen the water level. The mud was deposited on the north side, which is now dry ground. Today the park is managed by the Wright County Conservation Board.

DESCRIPTION: Covering 97 acres, Lake Cornelia Park is located on the northwest shore of the lake. There is a ranger in residence, and the park serves as headquarters for the Wright County Conservation Board. The lake covers 273 acres and was formed by a glacier during the Wisconsin Glacial Stage about twelve thousand years ago.

ACTIVITIES: Although some campers use a small area on the lakeshore, the 50-site campground is located to the north of the ranger's residence. Electrical hookups are available. The campground and the unsupervised beach for swimmers are heavily used during the summer. Near the beach are picnic areas and playground equipment. A baseball diamond is present, and the park has facilities for the handicapped. Snowmobiling is permitted in the winter. The lake has been stocked with walleyes, crappies, channel catfish, and bluegills. There is no size limit for boat motors.

The park is used for nature study, and a popular feature is the ¾-mile Behind the Scenes Nature Trail. The trail provides for observation of, and education about, local wildlife; marsh, upland prairie, and timber habitats; various trees, shrubs, and prairie grasses; and the conservation work that has been done.

ACKNOWLEDGMENT: Staff at the State Archives

FOR MORE INFORMATION:
Behind the Scenes Trail. Clarion: Wright County Conservation Board.

Lower Gar Access

LOCATION: ½ mile southeast of Arnolds Park on Highway 71 in Dickinson County

ADDRESS: Gull Point State Park, R.R. 2, Milford, Iowa 51351

TELEPHONE: (712) 337-3211 (Gull Point State Park)

DESCRIPTION: Lower Gar Access is a 7-acre picnic area offering public access to 273-acre Lower Gar Lake in Iowa's great lakes region. The area is located along the northwest shore of the glacial lake. Other state-owned parks and preserves in the area include Emerson Bay, Gardner-Sharp Cabin, Gull Point State Park, Isthmus Access, Marble Beach, Mini-Wakan State Park, Pikes Point State Park, Pillsbury Point, Trappers Bay, and Triboji Beach.

ACTIVITIES: The park offers fishing, picnicking, boating (no limit on size of boat motors), and snowmobiling when weather permits. Nearby are 310 acres open to hunting. The lake and upland habitats provide waterfowl, small game, and pheasant hunting.

FOR MORE INFORMATION:
Iowa Great Lakes Region. Des Moines: Iowa Department of Natural Resources.

Marble Beach State Recreation Area

LOCATION: 2 miles northwest of Orleans on Highway 276 in Dickinson County

ADDRESS: Gull Point State Park, R.R. 2, Milford, Iowa 51351

TELEPHONE: (712) 337-3211 (Gull Point State Park)

HISTORY: The area was named after the Marble family. William Marble was killed by Sioux Indians in March 1857 during the Spirit Lake Massacre. His wife, Margaret, was taken hostage but was freed two months later by other Indians.

171

DESCRIPTION: The 64-acre Marble Beach State Recreation Area is located along the west shore of Iowa's largest glacial lake, Big Spirit Lake. The area offers a panoramic view of the 4,169-acre lake. Other state-owned facilities in the area include Emerson Bay, Gardner-Sharp Cabin, Gull Point State Park, Isthmus Access, Lower Gar Access, Mini-Wakan State Park, Pikes Point State Park, Pillsbury Point, Trappers Bay, and Triboji Beach.

ACTIVITIES: Marble Beach has a very popular 224-site campground with modern restrooms, showers, and electricity at 100 sites. Unsupervised swimming, a boat ramp (no restrictions on horsepower), and picnicking are also offered. The lake is quite popular with boaters and fishermen due to its size and excellent water quality. A modern fish cleaning station is also present.

Hunting is permitted in the nearby wildlife area and on Spirit and nearby lakes. The area offers open timber and grassland habitats for water-fowl, squirrels, rabbits, and other animals.

FOR MORE INFORMATION:
Iowa Great Lakes Region. Des Moines: Iowa Department of Natural Resources.
The Spirit Lake Massacre. Spirit Lake: National Society Daughters of the American Revolution, Ladies of the Lake Chapter.

Mill Creek State Park

LOCATION: Just east of Paullina on Highway 10 in O'Brien County

ADDRESS: O'Brien County Conservation Board, Primghar, Iowa 51245

TELEPHONE: (712) 448-2254 (O'Brien County Conservation Board)

HISTORY: The land comprising Mill Creek State Park was purchased in the early 1930s by the citizens of Paullina at a cost of more than twenty thousand dollars. In December 1935, the land was deeded to the state for the purpose of developing a state park. Most of the development was done by the Works Progress Administration in 1937. Two of the original buildings are still in use.

In 1975 the O'Brien County Conservation Board took over management of the park. Three years were spent in dredging the lake of more than forty years of accumulated silt. Assisting in the project was a heavy equipment crew from Northwest Iowa Technical College. A siltation-prevention system was also implemented. Improvements in the park have been made with the assistance of the citizens of Paullina.

DESCRIPTION: The 124-acre Mill Creek State Park has a 25-acre artificial lake, Mill Creek Lake.

ACTIVITIES: The park offers a large campground (with electricity, modern restrooms, and showers), a playground, three large picnic areas, shelters, hiking trails, nature trails, nature study, an island for scout camping, a diving tower, a beach for swimming, and lake fishing (electric motors only).

ACKNOWLEDGMENT: W. L. Mau, executive director, O'Brien County Conservation Board, Primghar

Mini-Wakan State Park

LOCATION: 5 miles north of Orleans on Highway 276 to the Minnesota border, then east for less than a mile on a county road (Dickinson County)

ADDRESS: Gull Point State Park, R.R. 2, Milford, Iowa 51351

TELEPHONE: (712) 337-3211 (Gull Point State Park)

HISTORY: The site was a popular area with the Sioux and the Ioway Indians before white settlers arrived. Exactly when or how the lake was discovered by explorers is not certain, but Spirit Lake appears on maps as early as 1703. One theory is that Father Hennepin, a Franciscan missionary priest, visited the area in 1680 while he was a prisoner of Sioux Indians. The Indians knew the lake as "Water of the Spirits." They believed that vengeful spirits resided in the lake, waiting to kill anyone who ventured out onto the water.

The original 14 acres of the park were acquired by the state from J. H. and Maude McClelland on April 5, 1933, at a cost of $1,250.

DESCRIPTION: Mini-Wakan State Park is located just south of the Minnesota border and covers 20 acres along the north shore of 4,169-acre Big Spirit Lake. The lake is of glacial origin with numerous glacial boulders.

Other state-owned facilities in the area include Emerson Bay, Gardner-Sharp Cabin, Gull Point State Park, Isthmus Access, Lower Gar Access, Marble Beach, Pikes Point State Park, Pillsbury Point, Trappers Bay, and Triboji Beach.

ACTIVITIES: Because of its scenic location, Mini-Wakan is very popular for picnicking as well as fishing. A scenic stone shelter is available, as is a boat ramp. Perch, northern pike, bass, and other fish may be caught in Big Spirit Lake. A large fishing pier, accessible to the handicapped, is located nearby. There is no size limit on horsepower for boat motors. Snowmobilers, skiers, ice-skaters, and others who use the lake during the winter should be on the lookout for bubbles in the ice. These could indicate weak spots in the ice and are usually found off the points along the shore. The lake also offers waterfowl hunting.

ACKNOWLEDGMENT: Staff at the State Archives

FOR MORE INFORMATION:
Iowa Great Lakes Region. Des Moines: Iowa Department of Natural Resources.

Oak Grove State Park

LOCATION: 7 miles northeast of Hawarden on County Road K-18 in Sioux County

ADDRESS: Sioux County Conservation Board, Oak Grove State Park, Hawarden, Iowa 51023

TELEPHONE: (712) 552-1047 (Sioux County Conservation Board)

HISTORY: The original 77 acres of Oak Grove State Park were purchased on August 5, 1924, at a cost of eight thousand dollars. John Feikema first owned the land, and it had been a recreational area long before it was acquired by the state.

DESCRIPTION: About half of the park's 102 acres is comprised of rolling hills, and three-quarters of the park is densely timbered. The Big Sioux River runs adjacent to the park, and bluffs overlook the river. Iowa's oldest exposed bedrock, the Sioux quartzite (more than a billion years old), is exposed in the southwest corner of the park. The park also has the headquarters for the Sioux County Conservation Board.

FLORA: Most of the park is thickly timbered with oak, basswood, elm, maple, poplar, and other trees. Some prairie areas are also present and have an abundance of prairie grasses.

ACTIVITIES: The park has an excellent campground with electricity, modern restrooms, and showers. There are fishing and boating accesses to the river, hiking trails, picnic areas, and two shelters that are open to the public on a first-come basis. A third shelter has been developed into an interpretive center.

ACKNOWLEDGMENTS: Staff at the Sioux County Conservation Board, Oak Grove State Park
A. Dorothy Weiss, librarian, Orange City Public Library

FOR MORE INFORMATION:
Sioux County Conservation Board Parks and Recreation Areas. Oak Grove State Park: Sioux County Conservation Board.

Okamanpedan State Park

LOCATION: 3 miles northeast of Dolliver on County Road A-17 in Emmet County

ADDRESS: Fort Defiance State Park, Estherville, Iowa 51334

TELEPHONE: (712) 362-2078 (Fort Defiance State Park)

HISTORY: Lake Okamanpedan was first seen by the Frenchman Jean Nicollet, who surveyed the area in July 1838 for the federal government. The Indians called the lake "Okamanpedan," a Sioux name meaning "nesting place for blue herons." However, the birds abandoned the lake by the turn of the century. The name was adopted by the early settlers.

In 1924 E. L. and J. C. Williams donated 10 acres along the lake to the state for developing a park. In the 1920s, the state constructed a dam to raise the water level in the lake, which was stocked with fish. The park was

175

dedicated as Okamanpedan State Park on July 4, 1926, with 2,500 spectators on hand. A bronze plaque was placed in the park by the Okomanpado chapter of the Daughters of the American Revolution. Although the park's name has remained unchanged, the lake was later renamed Tuttle Lake in honor of Calvin Tuttle, who first settled here in 1856.

DESCRIPTION: The 19-acre park is located along the south shore of 981-acre Tuttle Lake. The shallow lake is the source for the east fork of the Des Moines River and lies on the Iowa-Minnesota border. In the vicinity is the Tuttle Lake marsh, which covers 160 acres. It is composed of river, upland, and wet meadow habitats.

ACTIVITIES: Okamanpedan State Park offers unsupervised swimming, picnicking, boating, and fishing. There is no size limit for boat motors. The lake itself is open to waterfowl hunting. Waterfowl, pheasant, deer, rabbit, and partridge may also be hunted in the Tuttle Lake wildlife management area nearby.

ACKNOWLEDGMENT: Carolyn Walz, librarian, Estherville Public Library

FOR MORE INFORMATION:
   Iowa Great Lakes Region. Des Moines: Iowa Department of Natural Resources.

Pikes Point State Park

LOCATION: 2½ miles southwest of the town of Spirit Lake on Highway 9 in Dickinson County

ADDRESS: Gull Point State Park, Rt. 2, Milford, Iowa 51351

TELEPHONE: (712) 337-3211 (Gull Point State Park)

HISTORY: The first 6.5 acres of Pikes Point State Park were acquired from several landowners on August 15, 1932. An additional 4.4 acres were purchased from Van Steinberg for $5,000, .33 of an acre from L. M. and Loretta Kuhn for $300, and 1.7 acres from Eugene Patterson and others for $2,445.

DESCRIPTION: Pikes Point State Park covers 15 acres and was acquired by the state to serve as one of the few public accesses to West Okoboji Lake, one of Iowa's premier natural lakes. The park is situated on the northeast shore of the 3,847-acre glacial lake.

Other state-owned facilities in the area include Emerson Bay, Gardner-Sharp Cabin, Gull Point State Park, Isthmus Access, Lower Gar Access, Marble Beach, Mini-Wakan State Park, Pillsbury Point, Trappers Bay, and Triboji Beach.

ACTIVITIES: The unsupervised swimming beach and the picnic grounds are popular attractions. An open picnic shelter is available. Snowmobiling and fishing are also popular. Common fish in the lake include walleyes, northern pike, smallmouth bass, white bass, perch, bluegills, crappies, catfish, bullheads, and muskies.

ACKNOWLEDGMENT: Staff at Iowa Department of Natural Resources

FOR MORE INFORMATION:
    Iowa Great Lakes Region. Des Moines: Iowa Department of Natural Resources.

Pillsbury Point Access

LOCATION: Off Highway 71 in Arnolds Park in Dickinson County

ADDRESS: Gull Point State Park, R.R. 2, Milford, Iowa 51351

TELEPHONE: (712) 337-3211 (Gull Point State Park)

HISTORY: Pillsbury Point was the site of the Spirit Lake Massacre in 1857 (see Gardner-Sharp Cabin Historical Site). The land had been owned by H. H. Lantz, who developed a recreation area here in the 1890s. When he died in 1925, his relatives donated part of the land to the state. An additional 2½ acres was purchased by the state in 1928 at a cost of $1,200. The park was named after Rev. Samuel Pillsbury, who owned the property in the 1860s.

DESCRIPTION: The park covers 6 acres along the southwest shore of West Okoboji Lake, a glacial lake of 3,847 acres lined with oaks and beautiful private residences. A museum is located here that recalls the Spirit Lake Massacre.

Other state-owned facilities in the area include Emerson Bay, Gardner-Sharp Cabin, Gull Point State Park, Isthmus Access, Lower Gar Access, Marble Beach, Mini-Wakan State Park, Pikes Point State Park, Trappers Bay, and Triboji Beach.

FAUNA: Wildlife areas in the vicinity are home to a wide variety of birds and other animals.

ACTIVITIES: The park offers picnicking, hiking, scenic views, unsupervised swimming, and fishing.

ACKNOWLEDGMENT: Staff at Iowa Department of Natural Resources

FOR MORE INFORMATION:
Iowa Great Lakes Region. Des Moines: Iowa Department of Natural Resources.
The Spirit Lake Massacre. Spirit Lake: National Society Daughters of the American Revolution, Ladies of the Lake Chapter.

Pilot Knob State Park and Preserve

LOCATION: 4 miles east of Forest City on Highway 9 in Hancock and Winnebago counties

ADDRESS: R.R. 1, Box 205, Forest City, Iowa 50436

TELEPHONE: (515) 582-4835

HISTORY: In August 1920, a public meeting was held in Forest City to discuss turning the Pilot Mound area into a state park. More than 150 citizens donated money to purchase the land at seventy dollars an acre. Matching funds were provided by the state. In 1921 the land purchase was approved, and, in 1924, the park was officially dedicated as Pilot Knob State Park. In 1934 several hundred members of the Civilian Conservation Corps came from Dolliver State Park to spend four months developing Pilot Knob. Present to celebrate the finished work on September 30, 1934, was most of the town of Forest City, including a band.

DESCRIPTION: Pilot Knob is a hill in the center of the park. When the

Pilot Knob State Park and Preserve

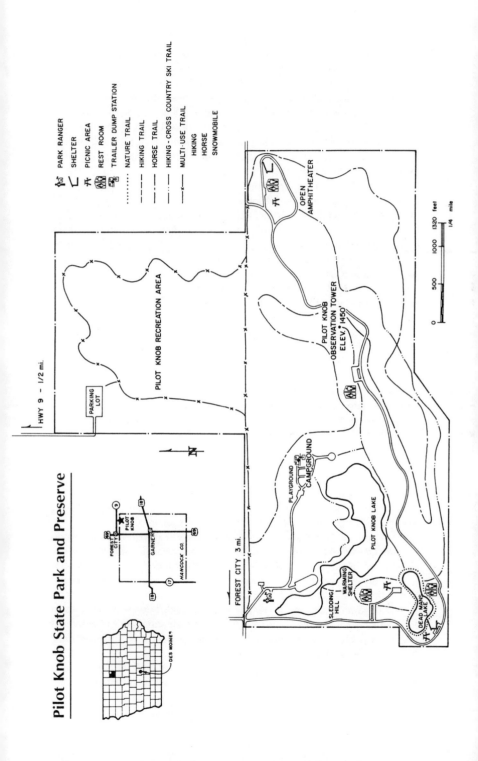

retreating glacier of the Wisconsin Glacial Stage halted temporarily about fourteen thousand years ago, sediment was allowed to build up, forming the knob and other smaller hills in the region. This was the last glacial advance into Iowa. The hill stands 300 feet above the Winnebago River. With an elevation of 1,450 feet, it is the second highest point in Iowa. On top of the hill is a beautiful 40-foot-high stone tower built by the CCC that provides views of the surrounding farmland and towns for a distance of at least 30 miles. Legend has it that pioneers on their way west used the knob as a landmark; hence the name, Pilot Knob.

In the southwest corner of the 700-acre park is spring-fed Dead Man's Lake, a name given to it by the Indians. It is shaped like a figure 8. The 5-foot-deep lake is unique in Iowa because of its high acidity. The lower half of the 8-acre lake is a floating sphagnum bog composed of living and dead plants. Although the existence of Dead Man's Lake has been known since the time of the early settlers, the significance of the bog portion of the lake was not known until 1954, when botanists R. F. Thorne and M. L. Grant discovered it. Only people with special permits to conduct scientific research or similar work are permitted onto the bog. A 369-acre portion of the park was designated a state preserve in 1968 because of Dead Man's Lake and other significant natural features. A hiking trail winds completely around the lake.

In the western part of the park is 10-acre Pilot Knob Lake. A heated "warming" shelter on the lakeshore provides comfort for winter sports enthusiasts. There are 4 miles of hiking trails and 4 miles of bridle trails in the park. The park has three picnic areas and an open picnic shelter located on the southwest end of Dead Man's Lake. The shelter may be reserved. An amphitheater is located in the eastern part of the park.

FLORA AND FAUNA: Dead Man's Lake harbors many rare plants and some invertebrates that are rarely found elsewhere in the state. No fish live in the lake. Three species of pond lilies may be found, including one found nowhere else in Iowa. The bog on Dead Man's Lake is surrounded by a marsh and is a popular area for waterfowl. Four species of sphagnum occur here as well as green algae, rare mosses, large-leaved pond weed, bog cotton, crested wood fern, black chokecherry, marsh cinquefoil, water shield, and bladderwort. The most unusual plant found here is the round-leaved sundew, which is not known in any other place in the state. Like the Venus flytrap, the sundew attracts insects and then slowly digests them.

Pilot Knob State Park is heavily wooded with twenty-five species of trees and several species of shrubs. There is also an abundance of wildflowers. Animal life is varied and numerous in the park, and includes deer, especially in the winter.

The McGrady Recreation Area lies on the north side of the park and offers hiking, snowmobiling, cross-country skiing, and public hunting.

ACTIVITIES: Pilot Knob State Park has an 80-site campground that is open year round, weather permitting. Electrical hookups, modern restrooms, and showers are available. The park's main road is closed in the winter but is open to snowmobilers. Also offered are scenic views, nature study, a nature trail, hiking, bridle trails, picnicking, playground equipment, bird-watching, and mushroom hunting. Pilot Knob Lake has been stocked with large-mouth bass, bluegills, and northern pike for fishermen. Only electric boat motors are permitted on the lake. Winter activities include ice-skating, sledding, snowmobiling, and cross-country skiing.

ACKNOWLEDGMENT: Barb Severson, Pilot Knob State Park

FOR MORE INFORMATION:
   Dead Man's Lake Self-Guided Interpretive Trail. Des Moines: Iowa Department of Natural Resources.
   Pilot Knob State Park. Des Moines: Iowa Department of Natural Resources.

Rice Lake State Park

LOCATION: 2 miles south of Lake Mills off County Road R-74 in Winnebago County (12 miles west of Interstate 35)

ADDRESS: Pilot Knob State Park, R.R. 1, Box 205, Forest City, Iowa 50436

TELEPHONE: (515) 582-4835 (Pilot Knob State Park)

HISTORY: Before the turn of the century, Rice Lake covered 500 acres. The marsh covered 700 acres, 200 of which contained wild rice. The lake and marsh were popular areas with fishermen and had an abundance of waterfowl and shorebirds. All but 60 acres of the area was drained in 1905 for use as farmland. Rice Lake went from a depth of 15 feet to a 4-foot-deep marsh.

   In 1924 the state purchased 14 acres along the south shore of the lake to develop a state park. The Rice Lake Outing Club donated an additional 22 acres. From 1937 to 1940, an additional 1,600 acres were acquired in the area by the state, with funding provided by excise taxes on guns and ammunition (the Pittman-Robertson Program).

   In the 1940s, many local citizens were not satisfied with the marsh and desired the lake to be deepened. Other citizens felt that the marsh was better for wildlife than a lake would be. The lake supporters were more convincing, and the water level was doubled from 4 feet to the present 8 feet.

DESCRIPTION: The present park covers 47 acres. It features an attractive and rustic picnic shelter and a pleasant walking trail. The lake covers 612 acres, is 8 feet deep, and offers bullheads and other fish for fishermen. A dam and a water control structure maintain part of the lake as a marsh.

A thousand acres of the area are timber and prairie habitats offering pheasant, rabbit, deer, and squirrel hunting. The 612-acre lake-marsh habitat offers waterfowl hunting. Six hundred acres along the west side of the lake serve as a refuge for waterfowl and are closed to the public from mid-September to mid-December. The eastern half of the lake lies in Worth County.

FLORA AND FAUNA: The area is rich in wildlife. Several islands in the lake contain native basswood and oak trees. Thousands of waterfowl migrate through here in spring and autumn.

ACTIVITIES: Rice Lake State Park offers picnicking, fishing, unsupervised swimming, bird-watching, a walking trail along the lakeshore, and a boat ramp. There are no restrictions on horsepower for boat motors. There is a shelter that is available to the public on a first-come basis. Hunting can be done nearby.

ACKNOWLEDGMENT: Barb Severson, Pilot Knob State Park

Stone State Park

LOCATION: Northern edge of Sioux City on Highway 12 in Woodbury County

ADDRESS: R.R. 3, Sioux City, Iowa 51103

TELEPHONE: (712) 255-4698

HISTORY: The land encompassing Stone State Park has been claimed in the past by Spain, France, and the United States. The area was a feeding ground for wildlife before settlers arrived, and several old trails beneath the

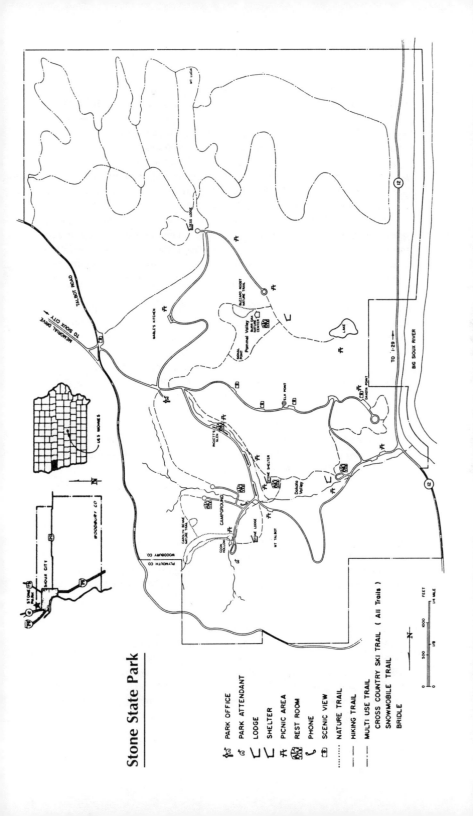

Stone State Park

dense brush are believed to have been made by buffalo. The last known wild buffalo in Iowa was killed here in 1868. The area was also popular with the Indians.

In 1895 Thomas Jefferson Stone, a banker in Sioux City, acquired the land. When he died in 1904, his son Edgar developed and used the area as a park until he died in 1911. His wife Lucia then donated Edgar's share of the land to the city in 1912. Sioux City purchased the other share from Edgar's sister, Alice. The city developed the 365-acre park, which included a zoo complete with bears.

In 1935 Sioux City donated the park to the state, mainly to obtain federal funds for the community during the Depression. All of the zoo animals were removed. During the late 1930s, the Civilian Conservation Corps further developed the park, which was named in honor of Thomas Stone.

DESCRIPTION: The 1,069-acre Stone State Park lies within the city limits of Sioux City (population 86,000), north of the junction of the Big Sioux and Missouri rivers. This is the westernmost state park in Iowa and is one of the most scenic. Stone Park is located in the unique loess hills of western Iowa. The loess hills were formed thousands of years ago by the deposition of windblown soil. The rugged and distinctive topography contains many plant species usually found in the more arid western states. The hills, indeed, resemble some of the "badland" areas of the western U.S.

In the northern area of the park are a rental lodge, Coon Hollow, Mount Talbot (named after Daniel Talbot, an early landowner), Dakota Valley, a nature trail, and the campground. In the central part are Signal Point, Pammel Valley, Mable's Kitchen, and a small lake. The southern part of the park has the Loess Lodge (available for rental); Mount Lucia (named after Edgar Stone's wife), elevation 1,410 feet; and bridle and snowmobile trails. Near the east entrance of the park is Mount Lookout. With an elevation of 1,472 feet, this is the highest point within the park. A road runs through the midsection of the park and provides several scenic views, especially from Elk Point and Dakota Point.

The Carolyn Benne Nature Trail includes stops at a marsh, a view of loess hills, a spring, a prairie grassland, and a scenic overlook of the Missouri and Big Sioux rivers. From here, visitors can see for 15 miles into three states—Iowa, Nebraska, and South Dakota. Also along the trail is an area that frequently has a multitude of fireflies in the summer.

Exposures of sandstone, shale, and chalky limestone of the Cretaceous period occur within the park, in an old quarry in the western area of the park, and along nearby Highway 12. Formations include the Dakota, Graneros, and Greenhorn. There are also loess, glacial till, and glacial boulders from the Kansan and Nebraskan glacial stages. In places, the loess is 50 feet thick.

FLORA AND FAUNA: More than seventy species of wildflowers occur here, including the yucca. A large portion of the park is heavily timbered with several types of trees. The park is home to most species of birds and animals that are native to Iowa, including the wily coyote.

ACTIVITIES: Stone State Park has 7 miles of roads, 20 miles of hiking trails, and some of the best bridle trails in the state. The bridle trails are open to snowmobilers in the winter, and cross-country skiers can use the roads and hiking trails. There is also an hour-long nature trail near the lodge at Coon Hollow. The Carolyn Benne Nature Trail is named after the person who designed it, Carolyn Benne. Within the park is a nature center (the Bur Oak Nature Center) that is open seasonally and by request for groups.

The park has six picnic areas; two lodges available on a rental basis; a 49-site campground with electricity (at 45 sites), showers, and modern restrooms; and several scenic-view sites. Fishing may be done in the nearby Big Sioux River and in a scenic pond within the park. Also offered are nature study and bird-watching.

ACKNOWLEDGMENT: Dale Brumm, park ranger, Stone State Park

FOR MORE INFORMATION:

Carolyn Benne Nature Trail. Des Moines: Iowa Department of Natural Resources.

Guernsey, N. F. *Geology of Stone State Park.* Sioux City: Newell F. Guernsey, 1983.

Guernsey, N. F. *History of Stone State Park.* Sioux City: Newell F. Guernsey, 1983.

Stone State Park. Des Moines: Iowa Department of Natural Resources.

Stone State Park: A Visitor's Guide 1984. Des Moines: Iowa Department of Natural Resources, 1984.

Trappers Bay State Park

LOCATION: Just west of Lake Park off County Road A-18 in Dickinson County

ADDRESS: Gull Point State Park, R.R. 2, Milford, Iowa 51351

TELEPHONE: (712) 337-3211 (Gull Point State Park)

HISTORY: Trappers Bay is the adjacent to Silver Lake, which was probably named by the Indians. The first settler here was George Nicholson in 1868. Another settler, Andrew Cloud, arrived here soon afterward. The area became a popular campground for trappers, hence the name. In 1933 the land was purchased from May A. Shriner by the state.

DESCRIPTION: Trappers Bay State Park is a 57-acre area along the north shore of Silver Lake. The 1,041-acre lake was formed by a glacier and is part of the Iowa great lakes region. Other state-owned parks and preserves in the area include Emerson Bay, Gardner-Sharp Cabin, Isthmus Access, Lower Gar Access, Marble Beach, Mini-Wakan State Park, Pikes Point State Park, Pillsbury Point, and Triboji Beach.

ACTIVITIES: The park offers picnicking, fishing, snowmobiling, and a boat ramp. There is no restriction on boat motor size.

ACKNOWLEDGMENT: Staff at Iowa Department of Natural Resources

FOR MORE INFORMATION:
Iowa Great Lakes Region. Des Moines: Iowa Department of Natural Resources.

Triboji Beach Access

LOCATION: Southeast of Montgomery on Highway 86 in Dickinson County

ADDRESS: Gull Point State Park, R.R. 2, Milford, Iowa 51351

TELEPHONE: (712) 337-3211 (Gull Point State Park)

HISTORY: The original Triboji Beach was a resort opened in 1929 by the old *Sioux City Tribune*. Five acres of the area were acquired by the state in 1982.

DESCRIPTION: The 5-acre access is situated on the northwest shore of West Okoboji Lake, a 3,847-acre lake formed by a glacier. Other state-owned facilities in the area include Emerson Bay, Gardner-Sharp Cabin, Gull Point State Park, Isthmus Access, Lower Gar Access, Marble Beach, Mini-Wakan State Park, Pikes Point State Park, Pillsbury Point, and Trappers Bay.

ACTIVITIES: There are docks and a lagoon built by local citizens, which are open to the public for fishing and unsupervised swimming. The park also offers picnicking, walking, and a scenic view. There is no size restriction on boat motors.

Twin Lakes State Park

LOCATION: 5 miles south of Pomeroy on Highway 4, then 3 miles east on Highway 124, in Calhoun County

ADDRESS: Black Hawk Lake State Park, P.O. Box 7, Lake View, Iowa 51450

TELEPHONE: (712) 657-2639 (Black Hawk Lake State Park)

HISTORY: The site of the present-day Twin Lakes State Park was originally known as "Sandy Point" and was owned by a man named Ramsey. It was a popular swimming area prior to becoming a state park in 1929. Local citizens had urged the state to purchase the property. During the 1930s, the Civilian Conservation Corps worked in the park. One of their projects was a rustic shelter that is available to the public on a first-come basis.

DESCRIPTION: The present park covers 15 acres along the east shore of North Twin Lake, with a few other smaller picnic areas around the lake. Both lakes are spring-fed and were formed by a glacier. North Twin Lake covers 574 acres, with a maximum depth of 13 feet in the southern part. South Twin Lake covers 600 acres but is shallower.

ACTIVITIES: Picnicking, unsupervised swimming, and fishing are offered, and the park is heavily used. A boat ramp is located to the south of the park. There is no size restriction for boat motors. Playground equipment is located within the park. There is a total of four shelters around the lake open to the public on a first-come basis. Hunting and fishing may be done on both lakes, but fishing is usually not as good on the south lake as it is on the north lake.

ACKNOWLEDGMENT: Eric Haakenson, park attendant, Black Hawk Lake State Park

FOR MORE INFORMATION:
Calhoun County History. Rockwell City: Calhoun County Historical Society, 1982.
Patterson, H. B. The Twin Lakes Story. Rockwell City: Golden Buckle Publishers, 1975.

Wanata State Park

LOCATION: ½ mile south of Peterson on a gravel road in Clay County

ADDRESS: Gull Point State Park, R.R. 2, Milford, Iowa 51351

TELEPHONE: (712) 337-3211 (Gull Point State Park)

HISTORY: The land was previously owned by the Northwestern Light and Power Company and was originally called Peterson State Park. It was dedicated on June 10, 1934, with 1,500 people in attendance. A band at the dedication was led by Karl King from Fort Dodge.

The park's name was later changed to Wanata to honor a Sioux chief. Chief Wanata was born near the Elm River in Brown County, South Dakota. He sided with England during the War of 1812. However, he had a change of heart around 1820 and became a friend to early pioneers. He died in 1848 in North Dakota.

DESCRIPTION: Wanata State Park is a 160-acre area along the Little Sioux River.

ACTIVITIES: The park offers picnicking and hiking. A scenic stone and timber picnic shelter is present.

ACKNOWLEDGMENT: Staff at the State Archives

Woodman Hollow State Preserve

LOCATION: Off County Road P-59 on the southern edge of Kalo, then less than 2 miles east on a gravel road, in Webster County

HISTORY: The land comprising Woodman Hollow State Preserve was purchased by the state in 1927 from the owner, A. S. Woodman. It was first developed as a state park. Latrines were built by the Works Progress Administration. However, the state later decided not to develop the site further but to leave it preserved in its natural state. Even the old latrines were not removed because doing so might have adversely affected the habitat. The property was dedicated as a state preserve on August 12, 1970.

DESCRIPTION: Woodman Hollow State Preserve is a 63-acre area of thick woods, prairie areas, and a ½-mile-long ridge that overlooks the Des Moines River. The view is most scenic in May and October.

A spring-fed stream has cut through the ridge of sandstone of the Pennsylvanian Period, Floris Formation. Near the western edge of the preserve, the stream drops about 12 feet. It joins the Des Moines River on the eastern edge of the preserve. Trees form a natural canopy over the hollow, whose sandstone walls reach up to 12 feet in height.

The access road has been closed, and the only remaining access is by hiking. The trails are not maintained but are the result of past visitors. At least forty-five minutes of hiking is required for the ridge trail, and the eastern end of the trail becomes quite rugged. A few miles to the south, along the Des Moines River, is Dolliver Memorial State Park.

FLORA: The preserve is home to many ferns, wildflowers, trees, shrubs, prairie grasses, and other flora, some of which are rare. The walls and the floor of the stream harbor one of the most varied, and perhaps densest, fern growths in Iowa. Ferns present include ostrich fern, spleenwort, woodsia, bladder fern, interrupted fern, rock-brake-fern, lady fern, maidenhair, and bulbet fern.

ACTIVITIES: Although not developed for recreational use, the preserve is an excellent area for nature study, scenic views, hiking, and photography.

ACKNOWLEDGMENT: Steve Bell, park ranger, Dolliver Memorial State Park

Appendix

Iowa's Geological Past

Little is known about the earliest period of Iowa's geological history, the Precambrian Period, which spans at least 4 billion years from the beginning of the earth to the start of the Cambrian Period (600 million years ago). Precambrian-Age boulders can be found in most of the state, brought here by the glaciers from areas farther north. There are a few exposures of Sioux quartzite, a reddish-colored metamorphic rock, in extreme northwestern Iowa (see Oak Grove State Park). Dated at around 1.5 billion years old, this is the oldest exposed bedrock in the state.

The early part of the Cambrian Period is absent in Iowa, but toward the close of the period, which ended 500 million years ago, various sandstones, siltstones, and dolomites were formed, and some of these contain marine fossils. The Cambrian marks the opening of the Paleozoic Era, when life became prolific on earth. Cambrian strata are exposed in the northeast corner of the state.

The Ordovician Period began 500 million years ago and ended 425 million years ago. Shales, limestones, dolomites, and sandstones are exposed in quarries, roadcuts, and along streams and rivers throughout northeast Iowa. Many of these exposures contain abundant and well-preserved marine fossils (see Pikes Peak State Park).

The Silurian Period (425 to 405 million years ago) is represented by dolomites and a few limestones exposed in the east central part of the state. Several of these formations are fossiliferous, and caves have been formed in some of these rocks (see Maquoketa Caves State Park). There are no Upper Silurian strata known in Iowa.

The Devonian Period began 405 million years ago and ended 345 million years ago. Limestones, shales, dolomites, and a siltstone were formed during this period in Iowa. Exposures occur throughout eastern portions and in the north central portion of the state. A wide variety of marine fossils (including fish teeth) can be found in abundance in many of these formations, and a few are widely known for their fossils, especially the Little Cedar, Coralville, Shell Rock, and Lime Creek formations. There are no Lower Devonian strata known in Iowa.

The Mississippian Period (345 to 310 million years ago) is represented

191

GEOLOGICAL UNITS IN IOWA

Note: With some exceptions, lines represent breaks in geological time.

System	Series	Group or Stage	Formation
		CENOZOIC ERA	
Quaternary (last million years)	Pleistocene	Holocene	recent deposits
		Wisconsin	Loess
			"Cary Till"
			"Tazewell Till"
		Yarmouth-Sangamon Paleosol	Sangamon Paleosol
			(Illinoian) Glasford
			Yarmouth Paleosol
		Pre-Illinoian	Wolf Creek
			Alburnett
		MESOZOIC ERA	
Cretaceous (middle) (135–65 million years ago)		Colorado	Carlile
			Greenhorn
			Graneros
		Dakota	Dakota
			Windrow
	Jurassic (180–135 million years ago)		Fort Dodge
		PALEOZOIC ERA	
Pennsylvanian (310–280 million years ago)	Virgilian (upper)	Wabaunsee	French Creek
			Jim Creek
			Friedrich
			Grandhaven
			Dry
			Dover
			Langdon (includes Nyman coal)
			Maple Hill
			Wamego
			Tarkio
			Willard
			Elmont
			Harveyville
			Reading
			Auburn
			Wakarusa
			Soldier Creek
			Burlingame
			Silver Lake
			Rulo
			Cedar Vale (includes Elmo coal)

System	Series	Group or Stage	Formation
Pennsylvanian (310–280 million years ago)	Virgilian (upper)	Wabaunsee	Happy Hollow
			White Cloud
			Howard
			Severy (includes Nodaway coal)
		Shawnee	Topeka
			Calhoun
			Deer Creek
			Tecumseh
			Lecompton
			Kanwaka
			Oread
		Douglas	Lawrence
			Stranger
	Missourian (upper)	Lansing	Stanton
			Vilas
			Plattsburg
		Kansas City	Bonner Springs
			Wyandotte
			Lane
			Iola
			Chanute
			Drum
			Cherryvale
		Bronson	Dennis
			Galesburg
			Swope
			Ladore
			Hertha
			Pleasanton (includes Exline limestone
	Desmoinesian (middle)	Marmaton	"Lost Branch"
			"Mound Valley"
			Lenapah
			Nowata
			Altamont
			Bandera
			Pawnee
			Labette (includes Mystic and Marshall coals)
			Stephens Forest
			Morgan School (includes Summit coal)

System	Series	Group or Stage	Formation
		PALEOZOIC ERA	
	Desmoinesian (middle)	Marmaton	Mouse Creek
		Cherokee	Swede Hollow
			Floris or "Spoon" (includes Carruthers and Laddsdale coals)
			Kalo (includes Cliffland and Blackoak coals)
	Atokan (lower)		Kilbourn
	Morrowan (lower)		Caseyville (includes Wyoming Hill and Wildcat Den coals)
Mississippian (345–310 million years ago)	Meramecian (middle)		Pella
			"St. Louis"
			Salem
	Osagean (middle)		Warsaw
			Keokuk
			Burlington
	Kinderhookian (lower)		Gilmore City and Maynes Creek
		North Hill	Starrs Cave
			Prospect Hill
			McCraney
Devonian (405–345 million years ago)	Upper	Yellow Spring	English River
			Maple Mill
			Aplington
			Sheffield
			Lime Creek
		Cedar Valley	Shell Rock
			Lithograph City
			Coralville
	Middle	Wapsipinicon Group	Little Cedar
			Pinicon Ridge
			Otis
			Betram
Silurian (425–405 million years ago)	Wenlockian (middle)		Gower
			Scotch Grove
	Llandoverian (lower)		Hopkinton
			Blanding
			Tete des Morts
			Mosalem

System	Series	Group or Stage	Formation
Ordovician (500–425 million years ago)	Cincinnatian (upper)		Maquoketa
		Galena	Dubuque
	Champlainian (middle)		Wise Lake
			Dunleith
			Decorah
			Platteville
		Ancell	Glenwood
			St. Peter
	Canadian (lower)	Prairie du Chien	Shakopee
			Oneota
Cambrian (600–500 million years ago)	Saint Croixan (upper)	Trempeauleau	Jordan
			St. Lawrence
		Tunnel City	Lone Rock
		Elk Mound	Wonewoc
			Eau Claire
			Mount Simon

PRECAMBRIAN ERA

(4 billion–600 million years ago)	Sioux quartzite

in Iowa by limestones, some dolomites, shales, sandstones, and a siltstone. Exposures occur in southeast and central Iowa. The majority of the formations are fossiliferous, and some are known worldwide for their fossils (e.g., Gilmore City, Maynes Creek, and Burlington). Plant fossils and rare amphibian fossils have been found in the "St. Louis" (being used with quotation marks by Iowa geologists until a more accurate name is found) Formation in Iowa. There are no known deposits of Upper Mississippian age (Chesterian) in the state (see Geode State Park, Oakland Mills State Park, and Starrs Cave Park and Preserve).

The Pennsylvanian Period began 310 million years ago and continued until 280 million years ago. Shales, sandstones, limestones, and coals were laid down throughout southern and central Iowa, representing a wide variety of environments. An abundance of flora and/or fauna occur in most of these formations. The oldest formations are exposed along the Mississippi River in the southeastern part of the state (see Wildcat Den State Park). The youngest formations are exposed along the Missouri River in southwest Iowa.

195

The Paleozoic Era closed with the end of the Permian Period, which lasted from 280 to 225 million years ago. It was during this period that the climate and life changed dramatically. Many of the marine organisms became extinct, and many of the land plants began to decline. New plants and animals began to appear during the Triassic Period, which opened the Mesozoic Era. Strata of neither period are known to exist in Iowa but are present in neighboring states.

The gypsum and associated shale and sandstone exposed in the Fort Dodge area are believed to have been formed during the later part of the Jurassic Period, which began 180 million years ago and ended 135 million years ago. Life during the Jurassic was very different than during the Paleozoic Era. Birds began to appear, and dinosaurs ruled the earth. However, the Fort Dodge Formation is devoid of fossils, except for some pollen and spores.

The Cretaceous Period (135 to 65 million years ago) marked the close of the Mesozoic Era. Exposures of Cretaceous sandstone occur in many areas of western Iowa and in a few areas in northern Iowa. The best exposures can be found in northwest Iowa, near the Big Sioux River. Here shales and a limestone are also present (see Stone State Park). The sandstone (Dakota) frequently has plant fossils, and dinosaur bones have been found recently in this formation, although they are rare. The limestone (Greenhorn) and shales (Graneros and Carlile) contain marine fossils (fish scales and teeth, and pelecypods).

The last 65 million years of geological history comprise the Cenozoic Era, which saw another major change in life. Many kinds of plants and animals, especially the dinosaurs, became extinct toward the close of the Cretaceous and were replaced by plants and animals that we are more familiar with. However, many of these early mammals are now extinct.

The Cenozoic Era began with the Tertiary Period (65 to 2.5 million years ago). Exposures of silt believed to be late Tertiary in age have been discovered recently in extreme western Iowa.

We live in the Quaternary Period, which began about one million years ago. In Iowa, the Quaternary Period saw the waxing and waning of glaciers, with at least four glacial advances into the state: Nebraskan, Kansan, Illinoian, and Wisconsin. Glacially transported material (till) and wind-blown silt (loess) were deposited throughout the state during this time. These are exposed in several state parks. Ice Age plants, mammals, and mollusks can be found in some of these deposits. Toward the close of the last glacial retreat, evidence of human habitation begins to appear in Iowa.

Fossils are still being formed today in Iowa. A good example are recent gastropods and blades of grass trapped in calcium carbonate precipitating from limestone bluffs (the same process that forms stalactites and stalagmites). The mineral solidifies and forms aragonite, preserving the organisms as fossils that can be as young as several hundred years.

FOR MORE INFORMATION:

Anderson, W. I. *Geology of Iowa*. Ames: Iowa State University Press, 1983.

Prior, J. C. *A Regional Guide to Iowa Landforms*. Educational Series no. 3. Iowa City: Iowa Geological Survey, 1976.

Rose, J. N. *Fossils and Rocks of Eastern Iowa*. Iowa City: Iowa Geological Survey, 1967.

Troeger, J. C. *From Rift to Drift*. Ames: Iowa State University Press, 1983.

Wolf, R. C. *Fossils of Iowa*. Ames: Iowa State University Press, 1983.

Iowa's Archaeological Past

The first evidence of human habitation in Iowa dates back to the last glacial retreat, about twelve thousand years ago. Known as the Clovis Culture, these people were nomads, hunting Ice Age mammals, especially mammoths, but also horses, camels, and bison. Clovis spear points have been found in Iowa, but most of our knowledge of these people comes from sites in western states. The culture was first studied at a site at Clovis, New Mexico.

After the Clovis people, there were several similar cultures from 9000 to 8000 B.C. They are named after their distinctive spear points and include Folsom, Hell Gap, Agate Basin, Eden, and others. These peoples probably formed bands based on families. At times several bands would unite to form communal hunts. They hunted mainly bison. The mammals hunted by earlier peoples were now extinct.

By 8400 B.C., the Archaic Culture had appeared in the northeastern United States. These peoples were more diverse hunters than earlier cultures and also gathered seeds and vegetables. Unlike earlier cultures, they seemed to travel with the seasons, having summer camps and winter camps. This trait was strongly developed by about 2000 B.C.

The Archaic people used a wider variety of tools than earlier peoples, including the spear thrower, and were the first people in North America known to make baskets. Stone drills and bone whistles have been found at some sites, and they may have been the first to use burial mounds. They are known to have driven entire herds of bison over cliffs in mass killings. The Archaic peoples were also the first to develop pottery (about 2000 B.C.).

197

The Archaic Culture ended around 1000 B.C. in eastern North America but may have continued about another thousand years in the Iowa area. During this time, there was a culture in the Great Lakes region (Old Copper Culture, 500 to 200 B.C.) that collected raw copper from the south shore of Lake Superior. They hammered the copper into ornaments, projectile points, and other artifacts. Some of these artifacts have been found at late Archaic sites in Iowa.

The Woodland Period began around 1000 B.C. in eastern North America and lasted until about A.D. 1000, when these people blended in with other groups. The Woodland people were the first to use pottery extensively, the first to construct burial mounds in large numbers, and the first to use pipes and tobacco.

Around 300 B.C. an elaborate cultural system was being developed in the Ohio area, the Hopewell Culture. From Ohio, they spread as far northeast as New York, as far southeast as Florida, and as far west as Kansas. The culture may have begun in Illinois or it may have emerged from the Adena Culture, which began in the Ohio region about 800 B.C.

Two major Hopewell centers are known, one in south central Ohio and the other along the Central Illinois River in Illinois. They developed additional complexes in northern Minnesota, Wisconsin, Missouri, and Oklahoma.

The Hopewell people buried their dead in mounds overlooking rivers. Later mounds include "effigy" mounds. About 200 B.C., the Hopewell people began constructing large mounds overlooking the Mississippi River. Several of the mounds contained elaborate offerings buried with the dead, probably members of the religious class. Burial mounds found to the west of the Mississippi in Iowa (i.e., along the Des Moines, Skunk, Iowa, and Cedar rivers) lack the elaborate offerings.

Hopewell people did some farming of corn and other crops, but their diet was mainly wild game (squirrels, deer, turkeys, and migratory birds), as well as plants and nuts.

They traded extensively, obtaining obsidian from Yellowstone, copper from the Great Lakes, mica from North Carolina, flint from North Dakota, and marine shells from the Gulf of Mexico.

By A.D. 400, the Hopewell Culture was declining. Their well-established trade structure broke down, and more isolated, smaller groups emerged. During this time, corn, beans, and pumpkins were introduced into the state, and the people began to use the bow and arrow.

In Iowa, the Archaic Culture may have merged with the Middle Woodland Hopewell Culture about A.D. 1. There is very little evidence of Early Woodland Culture in Iowa. However, there are several Middle Woodland sites, such as the Toolesboro Indian mounds (see Odessa Campground). The transition from Middle Woodland to Late Woodland occurred about A.D. 500.

The Late Woodland Culture apparently broke up into smaller groups around A.D. 1200, although some researchers believe that it continued until A.D. 1600. There were several Late Woodland peoples existing in the Iowa area. The "Sterns Creek" and "Missouri Bluffs" peoples lived along the Missouri River.

Located in Wisconsin, Minnesota, Illinois, and Missouri, along the Mississippi River, was the Mississippian Culture (which began around A.D. 800). They built earthen pyramids with flat tops that served as foundations for temples. None have been found in Iowa, but they are present in states to the southeast and east. The largest of these mounds is located at Cahokia, near East St. Louis. It measures 100 feet high, 700 feet wide, and 1,000 feet long, covering 16 acres. The culture thrived until about A.D. 1400 but may have continued on until the arrival of the Europeans in the 1700s.

The Effigy Mounds Culture is most noted for its effigy mounds. These people also left campsites, chipping stations (where tools were made), rock shelters, and villages. They appeared around A.D. 650, probably developing from an earlier Woodland Culture in Wisconsin, and continued until A.D. 1200. There is evidence, however, that they may have survived until 1642 in Wisconsin.

These people built extensive groups of mounds in Iowa. At least 374 effigy mounds were once present in Iowa, although only 46 remain today. In 1892, near Harpers Ferry, 174 effigy mounds were identified, along with 700 other mounds. However, the site has been virtually destroyed.

The Effigy Mounds people used the bow and arrow and cultivated corn and sunflower seeds. Unlike the Hopewell Culture, the Effigy Mounds Culture evidently lacked social classes. None of the mounds seem to contain anything of significantly greater value than any other mounds.

The Mill Creek Culture was located in northwest Iowa. It was more developed than neighboring cultures of its time and was strongly influenced by the Mississippian Culture to the east. It is possible that these people traveled to the Big Sioux and Little Sioux rivers from Aztalan in southern Wisconsin or Cahokia in southern Illinois (both Mississippian Culture centers).

By A.D. 900 the Mill Creek people were in northwest Iowa and trading with neighboring cultures, especially the Great Oasis. Shells from the Gulf of Mexico have been found at some sites. The people lived in settlements for a long period of time, producing a wide variety of artifacts, and occasionally even resettled previously abandoned settlements. Many of their settlements were fortified.

Mill Creek people hunted, fished, trapped, gathered, and cultivated corn, beans, and squash. Evidently, they even ate rodents.

A Mill Creek fortified village was discovered at the Wittrock site in northwest Iowa (Wittrock State Preserve). The settlement had ramps and bastions. The houses were large rectangular structures built of mud walls and grass roofs.

By A.D. 1400 the Mill Creek people had moved out of Iowa, leaving no clues as to where they went. Why they moved may have something to do with the Oneota people, who lived to the south. Because there was very little trading between these two cultures, and because of the Mill Creek's fortified villages, it is believed that the two peoples were enemies.

The Glenwood people (Nebraska Culture) were established in the Glenwood, Iowa, and southeast Nebraska area by A.D. 900. They were linked closely with the Mississippian Culture, but unlike some other peoples, they did not travel much, living and hunting in a relatively fixed area. They also traded very little with their neighbors, although in later stages of their culture, they did develop more trade with the Oneota Culture in Iowa, the Upper Republican Culture to the west, and the Mississippian Culture to the east.

The Glenwood people were peaceful groups that lived in 30-foot-square huts with walls made of vertical poles and sod roofs. In some places, they established small, unprotected communities. They supported themselves by growing corn, beans, squash, and probably tobacco, and by hunting deer, elk, bison, and other animals.

By A.D. 1400 (in the early stages of the late prehistoric period), the Glenwood people had evidently moved away and become integrated with other peoples.

The Great Oasis people were named after Lake Great Oasis, an ancient lake formed in Minnesota by the last glacial retreat. These people appeared along the lake by A.D. 900 and remained until A.D. 1300, surviving into the late prehistoric period. Probably descendants from earlier Woodland peoples, the Great Oasis people spread from Minnesota into Iowa, southeast Nebraska, and South Dakota. In Iowa, the Great Oasis people lived alongside the Glenwood, Mill Creek, and Oneota peoples. They did not seem to have been strongly influenced by the other cultures, but they did trade with the Mill Creek Culture and had access to shells from the Gulf of Mexico.

The Great Oasis people lived in villages of houses measuring 25 feet by 40 feet, constructed of vertical poles with thatch roofs. They used the bow and arrow and ate a wide variety of wildlife (especially deer and elk, but also clams, frogs, turtles, birds, fish, bison, rabbits, and possibly snakes). They also cultivated crops.

Near the close of the Late Woodland Culture (around A.D. 1000), the Oneota Culture appeared and continued into the late prehistoric period (which began around A.D. 1200). The Oneota may have originated in Cahokia in Illinois, which at that time was a religious and cultural center spanning an area comparable in size to New York City today. By A.D. 1150 the center was on the decline. Another theory is that the Oneota were descendants of an earlier Woodland people. The culture was named after the Oneota River (now the Upper Iowa River) in northeast Iowa, along which an Oneota site had been studied as early as 1914.

The culture spread across Minnesota, Wisconsin, Illinois, Missouri, eastern Nebraska, and Iowa. By A.D. 1200 to 1250, the climate in Iowa became drier and warmer, especially in the summer. The Oneota people then depended more upon hunting and less on farming. Their Late Woodland neighbors (Great Oasis, Mill Creek, Glenwood, and others) apparently were not able to adjust as well.

Oneota villages in Iowa were large (some covered 100 acres), and they were usually located along or near major rivers. Dead were buried in mounds near the villages, sometimes in mounds left by earlier peoples.

Until about A.D. 1350, the Oneota lived in northwest Iowa but traded very little with other cultures in that area (Great Oasis, Mill Creek), with the exception of the Glenwood people. They were better farmers than Late Woodland peoples, raising corn, squash, beans, and probably tobacco. The Oneota people hunted deer and bison mainly, and they fished and gathered seeds and nuts as well. They worked the Pipestone quarries in southwest Minnesota, using the stone called "catlinite" to make pipes and plaques. A wide variety of pottery has been found at Oneota sites, and it seems to vary from household to household.

Unlike most earlier cultures (with the exception of the Mill Creek) that consisted of hunting and gathering bands, the Oneota people developed into smaller tribes, especially during bad weather, but then recombined into villages during warmer months.

It is believed that the Mill Creek and Oneota peoples were enemies. There was no trading between the two cultures, and the Mill Creek people built fortified villages. When the Mill Creek people moved out of northwest Iowa (around A.D. 1300), the Oneota people took over their territory.

By A.D. 1200 the Oneota Culture was well established in three other areas of the state: in the vicinity of the present Red Rock Lake, along the Mississippi River and its tributaries (Des Moines, Skunk, and Iowa rivers) in southeast Iowa, and along the Upper Iowa River (about A.D. 1000) in northeast Iowa.

The Oneota group near Red Rock Lake did not reside there long. The site was located south of a Great Oasis site that existed in the Des Moines area from A.D. 900 to 1275. For a while, the two groups were probably contemporaneous, but the Oneota group left soon afterward, probably for southeast Iowa.

By about A.D. 1550, the Oneota groups in Iowa evidently had consolidated. It is not known what happened to the Oneotas, but they may have been the forerunners of the Ioway Indians. By A.D. 1700 European explorers were trading with Indians in the Iowa area who called themselves "Ioway." European artifacts have been found at Ioway sites in Clay, Dickinson, and Lyon counties. The first recorded contacts between the Europeans and the Ioways occurred in western Wisconsin and northeastern Iowa in the 1670s and 1680s (see Odessa Campground). The Ioway were present throughout Iowa by this time.

The Chippewa, Pottawattamie, and Winnebago Indians are believed to have developed from the Oneota Indians in Wisconsin, as did the Oto in Iowa, and other groups in neighboring states.

In 1830 the Ioway signed a treaty with the federal government, and they were moved to Missouri, and later into Kansas. By the turn of the century, the Ioway tribe had broken up and disappeared.

Little is known about the history of many Indian groups that were temporary residents of Iowa, such as the Sioux, Pawnee, Omaha, and Kickapoo, and not much more is known about native groups such as the Ioway and Oto.

Our knowledge of the Mesquakie Indians' history is more clear because the tribe still resides in the state. The first contact with Mesquakie Indians occurred near the present-day Green Bay, Wisconsin, in 1634. French explorers encountered a tribe who identified themselves as Fox. Actually, they were of the Mesquakie tribe, but members of the Fox clan.

The Mesquakie and their allies, the Sauk (Sac), did not get along with the French explorers, and they moved south, following the Mississippi River. By 1760 they had established permanent settlements from Minnesota to Missouri along the river. The Mesquakie settled on the Iowa side of the river. The Sauk settled on the Illinois side. Their main village, Saukenuk, was located east of the present-day Davenport. During the winter, the groups broke up, some going west to hunt bison. In spring, the villages would again become centers of activity.

In 1804 the Mesquakie were coerced into signing over their land to the government, even though the tribe members involved had no authority in the tribe to sign such an agreement.

The Mesquakie and Sauk continued to live in the area for twenty-five years, until the arrival of settlers pushed the Sauk Indians across the Mississippi River to join their Mesquakie neighbors on the Iowa side.

Chief Black Hawk of the Sauk rebelled and frequently returned to Saukenuk. The government prohibited his return in 1831. Black Hawk ignored the order, but upon his return in 1832, he found the village in ruins. He then sought help from the British and fellow Sauk Chief Keokuk in his showdown with federal troops. The aid did not materialize during a series of clashes known as the "Black Hawk War" (1832). With the troops in pursuit, Black Hawk fled his band, hoping that they would be spared. However, the Indians were killed, and Black Hawk was soon captured.

In 1833 President Andrew Jackson granted the chief a pardon, and he was permitted to live out his final years in Iowa.

The Mesquakie and Sauk signed additional treaties with the government in 1842, 1843, and 1845 that eventually placed the two groups in Kansas. Several Mesquakies, including Chief Poweshiek, remained in Iowa, living along the Iowa and Des Moines rivers.

Conditions in Kansas were harsh, and soon after 1845, the Mesquakies began to drift back to Iowa. In 1856 the Iowa legislature permitted the Mesquakie to stay. By 1859 they had purchased property in Tama County and formed a permanent settlement, where they still live today.

(Condensed in part from *Western Iowa Prehistory* (1975), and *Eastern Iowa Prehistory* (1981), both by D. Anderson and both published by the Iowa State University Press. Used with permission.)

FOR MORE INFORMATION:

Anderson, D. *Western Iowa Prehistory.* Ames: Iowa State University Press, 1975.

Anderson, D. *Eastern Iowa Prehistory.* Ames: Iowa State University Press, 1981.

Archaic Period. Educational Series no. 2. Iowa City: Office of the State Archaeologist.

Oneota. Educational Series no. 6. Iowa City: Office of the State Archaeologist.

Paleo-Indian Period. Educational Series no. 1. Iowa City: Office of the State Archaeologist.

Woodland. Educational Series no. 3. Iowa City: Office of the State Archaeologist.

Iowa Archaeological Society
117 East Willow
Cherokee, IA 51012

Office of the State Archaeologist
Eastlawn
University of Iowa
Iowa City, IA 52242

Further Reading

Dinsmore, J. J., T. H. Kent, et al. *Iowa Birds*. Ames: Iowa State University Press, 1984.

Discovering Iowa Treasures. Des Moines: Bureau of Tourism and Visitors, Iowa Department of Economic Development, 1988.

Harlan, J. R., and E. B. Speaker. *Iowa Fish and Fishing*. Des Moines: State of Iowa, 1956.

Iowa Conservation "in a Nutshell." Des Moines: Iowa Department of Natural Resources.

Iowa Conservationist. Des Moines: Iowa Department of Natural Resources, monthly.

Iowa Mammals. Des Moines: Iowa Department of Natural Resources.

Iowa Woodland Flowers. Des Moines: Iowa Department of Natural Resources.

Knudson, G. E. *A Guide to the Upper Iowa River*. Decorah: Luther College Press, 1971.

Musgrove, J. W., and M. R. Musgrove. *Waterfowl in Iowa*. Des Moines: State of Iowa, 1961.

Pratt, L. G. *Discovering Historic Iowa*. Des Moines: Iowa Department of Public Instruction, 1972.

Runkel, S. T., and A. F. Bull. *Wildflowers of Iowa Woodlands*. Des Moines: Wallace Homestead Book Company, 1979. Reprint. Ames: Iowa State University Press, 1987.

Van Der Linden, P. J., and D. R. Farrar. *Forest and Shade Trees of Iowa*. Ames: Iowa State University Press, 1984.

Index